ANGELINA JOLIE

ANGELINA JOLIE

A Biography

Kathleen Tracy

GREENWOOD BIOGRAPHIES

GREENWOOD PRESS
WESTPORT, CONNECTICUT • LONDON

Library of Congress Cataloging-in-Publication Data

Tracy, Kathleen.
   Angelina Jolie : a biography / Kathleen Tracy.
     p. cm. — (Greenwood biographies, ISSN 1540–4900)
   Includes bibliographical references and index.
   ISBN 978–0–313–36460–0 (alk. paper)
   1. Jolie, Angelina, 1975–   2. Motion picture actors and actresses—United
States—Biography.   I. Title.
   PN2287.J583T73   2009
   791.4302'8092—dc22
   [B]   2008038756

British Library Cataloguing in Publication Data is available.

Library of Congress Catalog Card Number: 2008038756

ISBN: 978–0–313–36460–0
ISSN: 1540–4900

First published in 2009

Greenwood Press, 88 Post Road West, Westport, CT 06881
An imprint of Greenwood Publishing Group, Inc.
www.greenwood.com

Printed in the United States of America

The paper used in this book complies with the
Permanent Paper Standard issued by the National
Information Standards Organization (Z39.48-1984).

10 9 8 7 6 5 4 3 2 1

CONTENTS

Photo essay follows page 42

SERIES FOREWORD

In response to high school and public library needs, Greenwood developed this distinguished series of full-length biographies specifically for student use. Prepared by field experts and professionals, these engaging biographies are tailored for high school students who need challenging yet accessible biographies. Ideal for secondary school assignments, the length, format and subject areas are designed to meet educators' requirements and students' interests.

Greenwood offers an extensive selection of biographies spanning all curriculum-related subject areas including social studies, the sciences, literature and the arts, history and politics, as well as popular culture, covering public figures and famous personalities from all time periods and backgrounds, both historic and contemporary, who have made an impact on American and/or world culture. Greenwood biographies were chosen based on comprehensive feedback from librarians and educators. Consideration was given to both curriculum relevance and inherent interest. The result is an intriguing mix of the well known and the unexpected, the saints and sinners from long-ago history and contemporary pop culture. Readers will find a wide array of subject choices from fascinating crime figures like Al Capone to inspiring pioneers like Margaret Mead, from the greatest minds of our time like Stephen Hawking to the most amazing success stories of our day like J.K. Rowling.

While the emphasis is on fact, not glorification, the books are meant to be fun to read. Each volume provides in-depth information about the subject's life from birth through childhood, the teen years, and adulthood.

A thorough account relates family background and education, traces personal and professional influences, and explores struggles, accomplishments, and contributions. A timeline highlights the most significant life events against a historical perspective. Bibliographies supplement the reference value of each volume.

TIMELINE: EVENTS IN THE LIFE OF ANGELINA JOLIE

1975	Born June 4 in Los Angeles to Jon Voight and Marcheline Bertrand
1978	Moves to Snedens Landing with her mom after parents' divorce
1982	Appears in her first movie *Lookin' To Get Out*
1986	Moves back to Los Angeles
	Attends Lee Strasberg Theatre Institute
1988	Starts experimenting with cutting herself
1991	Graduates from Beverly Hills High School
	Begins modeling
1993	Plays Casella "Cash" Reese in *Cyborg 2*
1994	Appears in *Meat Loaf: Bat Out of Hell* music video
	Begins affair with Jenny Shimizu
1995	Plays Kate Libby opposite Jonnhy Lee Miller in *Hackers*
	Stars in *Without Evidence* as Jodie Swearingen
1996	Co-stars in *Foxfire* as Margaret "Legs" Sidowski
	Plays Gina Malacici in *Love is All There Is*
	Plays Eleanor "Elie" Rigby in *Mojave Moon*
	Marries Jonny Lee Miller on March 28
1997	Plays Georgia Virginia Lawshe Woods in *True Women* on CBS
	Co-stars as Cornelia Wallace in *George Wallace*
	Appears in *Playing God* as Claire
	Enrolls in New York University's film school
1998	Dates Timothy Hutton
	Plays Gia Marie Carangi in TV Movie *Gia*
	Stars as Joan in *Playing by Heart*

Appears in *Hell's Kitchen* as Gloria McNeary

Nominated for both Lead Actress (*Gia*) and Supporting Actress (*George Wallace*) Emmys

Wins Golden Globe for *George Wallace*

Wins National Board of Review award for Breakthrough Performance in *Playing by Heart*

1999   Divorced from Miller on February 3

Plays Mary Bell in *Pushing Tin*, where she meets Billy Bob Thornton

Co-stars with Denzel Washington in *The Bone Collector*

Plays Lisa Rowe in *Girl, Interrupted*

Wins Golden Globe for *Gia*

Wins SAG Award for *Gia*

2000   Marries Billy Bob Thornton on May 5

Named one of People Magazine's 50 Most Beautiful People

Plays Sara "Sway" Wayland in *Gone in 60 Seconds* opposite Nicholas Cage

Wins Best Supporting Actress Oscar for *Girl, Interrupted*

Wins Golden Globe for *Girl, Interrupted*

Wins Actress of the Year at Hollywood Film Festival

Wins SAG Award for *Girl, Interrupted*

2001   Stars as Lara Croft in *Tomb Raider*

Plays Julia Russell in *Original Sin*

In August is appointed Goodwill Ambassador for the United Nations High Commission for Refugees

In September donates $1 million to help Afghan refugees

2002   Plays Lanie Kerrigan in *Life or Something Like It*

Announces adoption of Maddox Chivan Jolie on March 12

Files for divorce from Thornton on July 22

Legally drops "Voight" as surname on September 18

Earns Saturn Award Best Actress nomination for *Tomb Raider*

2003   Stars in Lara Croft sequel, *The Cradle of Life*

Suffers public estrangement from her father in August

Notes from My Travels is published by Pocket Books

Plays Sara Jordan in *Beyond Borders*

Given the first United Nations Correspondents Association Citizen of the World Award in October

2004   Plays Illeana in *Taking Lives*

Provides the voice of Lola in *Shark Tail*

Appears as Frankie in *Sky Captain and the World of Tomorrow*

Plays Olympias in *Alexander*

Photographed with Brad Pitt in Italy on location for *Mr. & Mrs. Smith*

2005   *Mr. & Mrs. Smith* released

Becomes third actress to earn $20 million for *Mr. & Mrs. Smith*

Earns Saturn Award Best Supporting Actress nomination for *Sky Captain and the World of Tomorrow*

Wins People's Choice Award for Favorite Female Action Movie Star

Wins Teen Choice Award for *Mr. & Mrs. Smith*

Adopts Ethiopian orphan Zahara Marley Jolie on July 6

Is named "official Cambodian" by King Norodom Sihamoni for her humanitarian work

2006   Ranked #1 in E! Television's 2006 101 Sexiest Celebrity Bodies

Formally announces that she and Pitt are a couple on January 11 with announcement of her pregnancy

Wins MTV Awards for Best Fight in *Mr. & Mrs. Smith*

Shiloh Nouvel Jolie-Pitt born May 27

Plays Margaret "Clover" Russell in *The Good Shepherd*

2007   Mother Marcheline Bertrand dies of cancer January 27

Adopts Vietnamese orphan Pax Thien

Stars as Mariane Pearl in *A Mighty Heart*

Plays Grendel's Mother in *Beowulf*

2008   Earns Golden Globe for *A Mighty Heart*

Provides the voice of Tigress in *Kung Fu Panda*

Plays Fox in *Wanted*

Twins born July 12 in France

Chapter 1

IN THE BLOOD

In Hollywood, acting has often been a family affair—from silent film stars Dorothy and Lillian Gish, to The Marx Brothers, to modern-day parent-child thespians Martin and Charlie Sheen and Goldie Hawn and Kate Hudson. Indeed, by all appearances, entertainment runs in the blood. Yet even so, being a member of a successful acting family is no assurance that a journey to the silver screen will be either smooth or inevitable. This was certainly true for Oscar-winning actress Angelina Jolie. While she and her father, Oscar-winner Jon Voight, are one of the most successful family acts currently at work in Hollywood, their relationship and its effect on Angelina's career is complicated.

Children sometimes reject their parents' values, but they often share the same ambitions that caused the rejection in the first place. Perhaps in the end, this is nothing more than the apple not falling as far from the tree as it may have wanted to, or perhaps, for all our free will, we are still slaves to our blood ties.

Voight's career would have a significant influence on Angelina. He pursued acting with a single-minded purpose, which he demonstrated even as a young boy growing up in the New York City suburb of Yonkers. His father, Elmer, was a professional golfer and his mother, Barbara, was a housewife. Voight remembers his dad as a wonderful, strongly principled man. "He didn't tolerate dishonesty, didn't like liars and didn't suffer fools gladly. People loved him," Jon recalled.[1]

While Jon showed flair as both an athlete and an artist, he aspired to act, so after graduating from Washington D.C.'s Catholic University, Voight made the pilgrimage to New York City, where he took acting classes and began landing small acting jobs. Although he picked up odd jobs here and there, he frequently had to borrow money from his father. Nevertheless, Jon says that his dad was always supportive and understanding, which he now understands "was difficult in a certain sense for a parent. Because you never know if a kid is going to be successful."[2]

When his dad was struck by a car and killed in 1964, Jon went through a period of severe grief and loss. However, he knew his father would want him to continue, so rather than pack up and go home, he kept going on auditions and took any roles that came his way. Then, in 1967, he became famous.

His breakout role was in *Midnight Cowboy* as Joe Buck, a naïve male prostitute whose homoerotic relationship with his ad hoc pimp earned the film Hollywood's first X-rating as well as an Oscar for Best Picture. The movie's critical success gave Voight what he needed—an entrée into film casting offices. Unfortunately, Voight's professional success coincided with the demise of his first marriage to actress Laurie Peters, whom he divorced in 1967. Voight moved to Los Angeles to pursue his film career and was cast in a string of successful movies, including *Deliverance*, *Odessa File*, and *Catch 22*. He also remarried—this time to 20-year-old French actress Marcheline Bertrand.

In 1973, Bertrand gave birth to James Haven, who was followed two years later by Angelina Jolie, born June 4, 1975. The children's middle names were intentional—Marcheline and Jon foresaw a day when their children might want to pursue entertainment careers but not use the family name.

Although Marcheline gave up her acting career when Angelina was born, Jon became increasingly absorbed in his. He directed all his energies toward acting and this left him very little time for his family. When Angelina was just a toddler, Jon and Marcheline separated. Jolie calls her father the perfect example of an artist who couldn't stay married. She speculated that it scared him to have what many would see as the perfect family.[3]

Only 25, Bertrand found herself a single mom raising two young children. She and the children moved back to New York to settle in Snedens Landing, a picturesque community perched along the Hudson River.

A year after he and Bertrand separated, Voight won the Best Actor Oscar for his portrayal of a paralyzed Vietnam veteran in the 1978 film *Coming Home*. Despite winning an Oscar, Voight would go through lean times as an actor, made leaner because he seemed incapable of hanging on to money. He spent it as soon as he earned it, which is why he had never bought a house and why, until they separated, Marcheline and the kids had lived in what locals called the slums of Beverly Hills—neighborhoods of apartment houses that lay adjacent to the well-tended lawns of the expensive houses.

"My father was very uncomfortable about success," Jolie explains. "Like, somehow it was great to live without, to give away everything you had. You know, to have money meant that maybe you were a bad person or something."[4]

Looking back, Voight says that even as a child, there were indications of the person Angelina would grow up to be. "Everyone who has children knows that mysterious aspect before we program them to make our lives convenient," he claims. He says his daughter, who he sometimes calls Jellybean, was "a very bright baby. She always had so much to say, even before she could talk!"[5]

While he thinks they share a reflective, philosophical nature, Voight acknowledges that Angelina has always been fiercely independent. "Since she was a baby she wouldn't let you help her, even with her ABCs. She'd say, No! I do it. I do it," he recalls. "That's the way she is."[6] Angelina was also assertive and uninhibited. As a tyke in kindergarten she and some other girls formed a gang called the Kissy Girls. The girls would chase little boys, catch and kiss them, and then watch them holler. Also, Jolie recalls, "I had two good friends who became my boyfriends, and I think the school called my parents because we were in front of the school grabbing each other. Obviously that was disturbing to the parents and the people driving by."[7]

Jolie was also a natural performer. When she was seven, Angelina made her screen debut in the Hal Ashby-directed film Lookin' to Get Out, which her father starred in and also helped write. In the film, Jolie had a walk on bit, as did her mother, who was billed as "girl in jeep." Although Ashby and Voight created screen magic in Coming Home, Lookin' to Get Out was a complete flop. Not only did critics skewer it, it bled red at the box office, recouping only $300,000 of its $17 million budget. However, if there was a bright spot amidst the cinematic carnage, it was that Angelina loved being in front of the camera, and the camera loved her.

This was doubtless not a surprise to her father, who had always believed she was destined to be an actor—partly because she was a bit on the dramatic side and very creative. Jolie, too, remembers the thrill of attention she got from performing as a child. "I found that when I was four years old, there was this part of me that liked making people laugh and liked wearing glitter underwear. And how can you not?" she jokes.[8] "I used to wear costumes all the time. I had this black velvet frilly little showgirl thing with sparkles on my butt, and I used to love those plastic high heels. There's a picture of me having my five-year-old birthday party: I had curled my hair and put lipstick on, very girly," she laughs.[9]

In a 1997 *Interview* magazine interview conducted by her dad, Jolie would say, "God, my earliest memories are of my brother pointing the home video camera at me and saying, *C'mon, Ange, give US a show.* Neither you or Mom ever said, *Be quiet! Stop talking!* I remember you looking me in the eye and asking, *What are you thinking? What are you feeling?* That's what I do in my job now—I say, *OK, how do I feel about this?* And I immediately know, because that's how I grew up."[10]

Reflecting on her childhood from the perspective of a parent, she explains, "Artists raise their kids differently. We communicate to the point where we probably annoy our children. We have art around the house, we have books, we go to plays, we talk. Our focus is art and painting and dress-up and singing. It's what we love. So I think you can see how artists in some way raise other artists."[11]

However, while Angelina may have been destined to act, she would do it in her own way, with her own style. During adolescence, Angelina was a non-conformist. In a display of individuality, she dyed her hair blue and wore only studded jackets. "When we moved back from New York, I had gotten really into leather," she recalls. "I think I loved Michael Jackson or something. I used to wear the leather jackets with the zippers, or collars with studs on them, and I used to ask if I could go to school wearing studs."[12]

She was also a little bit dark. At one point, she considered becoming a funeral director. In a 1996 *People* interview, Jolie explained, "There's something about death that is comforting. The thought you could die tomorrow frees you to appreciate your life now."[13] But she does not see that as being morbid—quite the opposite. "I'm probably the least morbid person. I've kind of discovered that if I think about death much more than some people have, it's probably because I love life more than those people."[14]

One of Jolie's most vivid recollections of childhood is when her mom inadvertently introduced her to knives. "I went to the Renaissance Fair with my mom when I was a little girl and there were all these kinda *knives,*" she would later tell TV talk show host Conan O'Brian. "It reminds you of history and there's something really beautiful and traditional about them, and just different countries have different weapons and blades and there's something beautiful about them to me. So I began collecting knives—I've collected weapons since I was a little girl."[15]

Showing that she also marched to the beat of her own erotic drummer, Jolie admits that her first sexual fantasy revolved around *Star Trek*'s Mr. Spock. "I think a lot of women might agree with this because he's kinda reserved and he has that sense of, *You can't break through to me, and you can't touch me.* So he's a challenge, you know? You kinda like think, *Oh, I can get him.* There's got to be something underneath those ears and hair, and, yeah," she laughs, "it's kinda perverted."[16] Aside from Spock, Jolie was also intrigued by Vlad the Impaler—the Romanian ruler Dracula is based on.

When Jolie was 11 years old, Marcheline moved back to Los Angeles, making it easier for Voight to maintain contact with the kids.

When Angelina stayed with her dad on weekends, they would spend time on the beach and catch up with each other. Telling her she was his best critic, Voight would discuss potential movie projects at length, asking Angelina's opinion and declining to take roles she didn't approve. Jolie knew she loved expressing herself creatively, but she didn't know what career path she would take; at different times she envisioned herself being a writer or painter. Voight, however, seemed intent on reeling her in to the acting life.

However, despite his efforts to maintain a hands-on relationship with his children, the divorce still had a profound effect on Angelina and James. Also, because Angelina and her father shared many personality traits, the two of them would butt heads during her adolescence. "He wasn't like a dad," she explains. "He was this man I knew. He was a very complicated man and he always meant well and I always wanted to love him, but we both attacked each other because we both thought we were right about everything. We'd debate anything. But I love that. That's why I question everything. But . . . he wasn't there a lot, so I became strong for my mom."[17]

Additionally, Jolie struggled against the expectations people had about her because of her famous father. When you grow up in the land of mansions and your dad is an Oscar-winning actor, people make assumptions. "Everyone thought I had money," Jolie reflects. "I had to go to my teacher and say, *I can't keep redoing my papers because I don't have a computer.* And I remember the teacher saying, *Have your father buy you one.*"[18]

While her Beverly Hills High School classmates spent their ample allowances in Rodeo Drive boutiques, Jolie bought her wardrobe at thrift stores and in Gen-Xer areas like the Melrose district. Voight doesn't deny he wasn't the best financial provider for his children. "I went through some dramas," he admits. However, he considers those experiences useful. "I think as I look back, all of those times are of good use to me, because they taught me many things. And maybe taught my kids a few things as well. When they saw me struggle with different things, and all the real difficulties that I've had, if I shared them, they'd become lessons for them as well. So they can see, well this happened here, and this is the way that Dad responded to it. And if they know my weaknesses as well as my strengths, that doesn't hurt either."[19]

Whatever embarrassments she may have suffered for it, Jolie would eventually become pragmatic about her dad's foibles. She also acknowledges that she and her brother never lacked for anything and that their dad spent what little spare time he had with them.

Finances aside, Jolie later admitted that a main issue with her father was his leaving her mom when she and her brother were so young. However, Angelina struggled against those who assumed she must harbor unexpressed issues with her famous father. She recalls going to a therapist for extra credit in high school. "It was just a part of life studies, psychology. So I went. And I realized how dangerous these people could be," she explains. "This person kept talking about my feelings for my father. I'd say, *No, I'm not angry. I understand. I think my parents are both wonderful individuals.* And she just couldn't believe it wasn't a problem for me." One day at therapy, Jolie made up a dream about stabbing her father with a fork. She remembers her therapist said, "*Aha, I see.* And I thought, *You f***ing a**hole.*"[20] That was the end of therapy for Jolie.

While Angelina's relationship with her father played out in public, her mother also had great deal of influence during Angelina's formative years. Marcheline occasionally shuttled her children back and forth between New York and Los Angeles, but the West Coast was primarily home, and was the place Angelina would begin to strike out on her own.

When she was 14, she began modeling; her lanky body and exotic face made her a natural in front of the camera and through each step, Marcheline counseled and advised her daughter. She also set herself up as Jolie's manager and made sure Angelina, whom she nicknamed Bunny, was treated properly by the agents and photographers with whom she came into contact.

When she was 16, Angelina moved out of her mother's home and into a small, nearby studio. Always smart and articulate, Jolie had graduated from high school a year and a half early, which freed her to pursue any professional avenue she chose.

Whether because of her father's influence or because she was always destined to follow the acting muse, Angelina eventually began studying and training at the famed and exclusive Lee Strasberg Theatre Institute. "I didn't know exactly what I wanted, but I knew I didn't know any other way to express me," she reflects. "My way of explaining things to people is through emotions; to listen to people and feel things. That's what an actor is so I think that's why I had to do it."[21]

One of the first workshop performances she did there was from *Room Service*, the Marx Brothers movie. She auditioned to play the manager. "I thought I should play the role as this German dominatrix," she says. "My dad came to see this play to see what kind of an actor I was going to be or what kind of choices I was going to be making. And instead of seeing me come out as a sweet little girl or the sexy woman who's from out of town and staying at the hotel, I came in as this insanely driven, dominant person who everybody laughed at. That's when he realized, *she does share my sense of the bizarre.*"[22]

However, rather than immediately delving into the profession, Jolie backed off. She stopped acting to just hang out and enjoy being a teenager. During this time, however, she would visit her father every Sunday and read plays with him. Despite his belief that she was destined to act, the idea of his daughter choosing the acting life gave Jon some paternal pause. "He didn't want to send me off to do something unless it was something I really needed to do," Angelina explains. "He was worried that I was doing it just because I had grown up with it, and thought it would be easy. He knew it was a certain kind of a life, and hoped that I had what it would take to do it. He wanted me to fight it out, and prove it for myself."[23]

Before launching her screen career, Jolie also starred in music videos for Lenny Kravitz and Meatloaf, driving to the auditions and shoots in the Ford truck she bought with her modeling money. She also appeared in five student films her brother shot while he was a film major at the University of Southern California. Besides wanting the work experience, Angelina enjoyed being around her brother, who was as conservative as she could be wild. Not only did she consider him her best friend with whom she could talk about anything, she also loved his gentle side.

Angelina liked people who did things their own way and expected no less from herself, which is why one day she'd attend punk-rock shows and the next spend hours taking ballroom-dancing lessons.

She was also keen on distancing herself from the perception she was a Hollywood insider. In her mind, even her father was on the outside. When she was getting into the business in her late teens and early twenties, Voight was in one of his career dry spells; while he was respected as an actor, he wasn't being invited to any big premieres. Even so, Angelina was very sensitive to the idea that anyone might accuse her of taking advantage of the paternal family name. Early on, she made the decision to drop the name Voight, proving that at least in that case, Jon and Marcheline had been particularly prescient. "I'm my mother and my father's child and I'm also my own person," Jolie says. "From the very beginning, I didn't want to feel like I was walking into a room and automatically being compared to him, or feeling like I was being let into any rooms because of him."[24]

Nor did she want to be hired solely on the basis of her name. "I'm not ashamed of my background. I'm very proud of my father and the work he's done. But I don't want anyone to be expecting me to be him."[25]

Not to worry. As soon as Angelina hit the big screen, few would ever mistake her for her father. From the outset, it was clear that Angelina was going to be unique, both professionally and personally.

NOTES

1. Eric Harrison, "The Many Faces of Voight . . . ," *Los Angeles Times*, January 22, 1999, Calendar section, 2.

2. Prairie Miller, "Varsity Blues: Interview with Jon Voight," *Star Interviews*, January 1, 1998, http://www.highbeam.com/doc/1P1-20559900.html.

3. Dark Horizons, Paul Fischer, January 14, 2000, http://www.darkhorizons. com/interviews/angelina.php.

4. Deanna Kizis, "Truth and Consequences," *Harper's Bazaar*, November 1999, http://fansites.hollywood.com/~ajolie/int15.html.

5. Jeannie Williams, "Voight a Dad Close to His Own 'Babies'," *USA Today*, March 12, 1999, D1.

6. Larry Sutton, Ken Baker, and Champ Clark, "Ark de Triumph: Jon Voight Sets Sail on T.V. as Noah," *People*, May 3, 1999, http://members.tripod.com/ ~Monkees23/jvoight/jvpeopl.html.

7. Mimi Udovitch, "The Devil in Miss Jolie," *Rolling Stone*, August 19, 1999, http://www.rollingstone.com/news/story/5939518/the_devil_in_miss_jolie.

8. Christine James, "'Dancing' Queen Angelina Jolie Gets Constructive in *Dancing about Architecture*," *Box Office Magazine*, December 1998, p. 6.

9. Mimi Udovitch, "The Devil in Miss Jolie."

10. Angelina Jolie, "Angelina Jolie," interview by Jon Voight, *Interview*, June 1997, http://www.001pic.com/AngelinaJolie/interview.html.

11. Rich Cohen, "A Woman in Full," *Rolling Stone*, July 2008, http://www. 001pic.com/AngelinaJolie/interview.html.

12. Dany Jucaud, "And the Devil Created Angelina Jolie," *Paris Match*, February 17, 2000, http://angelanna3.tripod.com/interviews2000/id11.html.

13. "On the Move: Name Dropper Not Billing Herself as a Voight," *People*, July 8, 1996, http://www.people.com/people/archive/article/0,,20141730,00.html.

14. Mimi Udovitch, "The Devil in Miss Jolie."

15. Angelina Jolie, interview by Conan O'Brien, *Late Night with Conan O'Brien*, NBC, January 13, 2000.

16. Angelina Jolie, interview by Jay Leno, *The Tonight Show with Jay Leno*, NBC, January 29, 1998.

17. BeatBoxBetty, "Angelina Jolie—Girl, Interrupted," May 23, 2000, http://www.beatboxbetty.com/celebetty/angelinajolie/angelinajolie/angelinajolie.htm.

18. Deanna Kizis, "Truth and Consequences."

19. Prairie Miller, "Varsity Blues."

20. Alison Boleyn, "Celebrity Profile: Angelina Jolie," *Marie Claire*, February 2000, http://angelanna3.tripod.com/interviews2000/id7.html.

21. Jack Garner, "Jolie's Performance in *Playing by Heart* Is Drawing Attention," *Gannett News Service*, January 21, 1999.

22. "Dancing" Queen, November 1998, http://www.wutheringjolie.com/nuke/modules.php?name=Content&pa=showpage&pid=314.

23. Jack Garner, "Jolie's Performance."

24. Bert Osborne, "Interview with Angelina Jolie," *Jezebel*, February 2000, http://angelanna3.tripod.com/interviews2000/id7.html.

25. Jeff Strickler, "Actors Hope They Can Hack It: Cyber-Film Stars Faked Computer Skills," *Minneapolis Star Tribune*, September 10, 1995.

Chapter 2

LIFE LESSONS

As she matured, Angelina took on an exotic appeal that defied classic beauty, particularly as it is defined by Hollywood. Although slender, with almost spindly arms and legs, Angelina was also buxom and her head seemed just *this* too large for her shoulders. Her face, however, with its full lips and wide smile, was the darling of the camera lens. Despite this, when assessing herself, Jolie has commented that she has always felt as if she looked a little bit like a Muppet. Her favorite body part was also a bit atypical for a starlet—she liked her forearms because of the way her veins looked.

The modeling photographers' cameras seldom picked up the faint scar running along her left jaw-line. Although she has never gone into great detail, Jolie has acknowledged that the scar is the remnant of a youthful experiment with a knife and her then-boyfriend. It would not be the last time she was left scarred from such an experiment.[1]

When Angelina was 18 years old, she was hired for her first adult film role. The movie was 1993's sci-fi thriller, *Cyborg 2: The Glass Shadow*. In *Cyborg 2*, the year is 2074 and androgynous cyborgs have replaced humans in all levels of society. The plot centers on the ruthless dealings of the Pinwheel corporation, which has developed an explosive device called Glass Shadow. The device can be injected into cyborgs, which can then be used as unwitting assassins. The movie begins with Pinwheel executives reviewing a film of their explosive agent at work. A beautiful female android is having sex with her unsuspecting victim. Just as she reaches orgasm, she explodes, niftily blowing up her target and giving a whole new spin on *in flagrante delicto* (which in Latin means *while [the crime] is blazing*, but has come to mean getting caught having sex). Thanks to Glass Shadow, the evil powers at Pinwheel believe they now hold the combustible key to rule the world—or at least destroy their chief competitor.

Ready to implement their master plan, the corporation chooses Jolie's character, Cash Reese, as their ignorant assassin. Reese is initially unaware of the deadly fluid coursing through her cyborg veins, but when she discovers her potential fate, she turns to a human martial arts instructor for help. Together, they make their way to a "free zone" where Glass Shadow is rendered ineffective and they live happily ever after.

Like the original *Cyborg* film, which starred Jean-Claude Van Damme in a post-apocalyptic tale of evil gangs, *The Glass Shadow* was uniformly skewered by critics.

In her next film, Jolie was safe from the critics' gaze—but only because the film never secured a general release. 1992's *Without Evidence* was a kind of extended *America's Most Wanted*—a cinematic attempt to uncover information about the murder of Michael Francke, the Oregon Department of Corrections Director who was stabbed to death outside the Corrections Department headquarters in Salem, Oregon on January 17, 1989. At the time of his murder, it was widely rumored that Francke was about to expose corruption in the prison system. The film, written by Gill Dennis and *Oregonian*-columnist Phil Stanford, thus proposed that Francke's death was part of a political conspiracy and that an innocent man was imprisoned for his killing.

Authorities had arrested Frank Gable, a convicted drug dealer, and he was convicted of stabbing Francke in the heart when he attempted to break into Francke's car. Gable, who is now serving a life sentence without the possibility of parole, has always maintained his innocence, claiming the real killer was a man who died several years ago. As of May 2008, his case was in appeals and he had requested DNA testing that he claimed would prove his innocence.

While her first two films impressed neither critics nor filmgoers, they did show Angelina's willingness to do projects off the beaten path and also showed her ability to immerse herself in the role, regardless of how absurd the script or how small the film. In her next film, Jolie would not only get into the skin of her character, she would get under the skin of co-star Jonny Lee Miller.

Hackers (1995), was one of the first films to tap into the growing, global fascination with the Internet. The movie follows a group of high-school computer junkies who discover plans for an upcoming $25 million computer crime. The King and Queen of these cyberpunks are new-boy-in-town Dade (Miller), and Jolie's Kate, or as they are known online, Zero

Cool and Acid Burn. Dade comes on the scene with built-in credibility—as a kid, he hacked into over a thousand Wall Street systems. Although he was caught and ordered to stay away from computers until he was 18, Dade accidentally stumbles upon a computer virus of unprecedented proportions. The virus is created by a villainous, master hacker who calls himself The Plague and who works as a security consultant for a major oil corporation. The virus will wreak worldwide havoc within days unless The Plague is paid. When The Plague realizes he's been discovered, he frames Dade. What follows is predictable, but it's presented in a slick fashion, with plenty of computer graphics to add color and flash.

Ironically, both Miller and Jolie admitted to being completely computer-illiterate. Angelina seemed particularly proud of it. During a press junket interview to promote the film, she announced she hated computers. She also admitted they scared her and that she was always afraid of breaking them. Miller confessed he didn't own a computer and explained that while he appreciated their place in society, he didn't feel the need to chat online or browse Internet sites for information.

Instead, what appealed to Jolie and Miller was subversive quality of hackers, as well as their self-proclaimed role as defenders of true democracy. However, in contrast to the shadowy figures the movie portrays, Jolie claimed that hackers were really quite social. "You can call them nerds, but they are good nerds. So many people sit at their computers from 9 to 5 because that's their job. These guys do it because they love it," Jolie said at the time. Miller agreed and noted that hacking is less about stealing and more about uncovering hidden information; without hackers, Miller claimed, people would be completely at the mercy of large corporations.[2]

Jolie also thought that film was appealing because of the way it questioned conventional wisdom. "I think Hackers is about testing barriers, testing opinions," she explains. "It's not just testing the limits around masculine and feminine; it was about testing barriers about different races, different sexes." The experience was fun for her, she said, since the hacker culture allows people to experiment and do or be anything they want.[3]

Prior to the start of filming, Hackers-director Iain Softley gave Miller and Jolie a crash course on computers so he could be confident they wouldn't have to fake the computer scenes. Almost in spite of herself, Jolie was fascinated: "Even though I'm not into computers, part of me had fun. It's neat to push one little button and have everything happen—or have everything disappear."[4]

In addition to computer skills, the script necessitated a considerable amount of time on rollerblades. Rollerblading and hanging out with the cast was one of Jolie's favorite parts of the filming. The other cool part was getting to meet real computer hackers. While she says she didn't really know what a lot of the lines meant, the experience was still completely fascinating.[5]

In a case of cyber irony, MGM/UA, the studio distributing the film, was given a taste of real-life hacking several days prior to the film's release. Jeff Moss, who organizes hacker conferences, revealed to reporters that hackers who were hired as consultants on the film passed along copies of the screenplay to friends via the Internet. A group of hackers who felt the movie didn't do them justice were so annoyed they hacked into the MGM/UA web site and added a billboard that labeled the movie "lame" and "cheesy." They also defaced pictures of the actors and replaced publicity shots with a snapshot of real hackers drinking beer.

The prank delighted the studio, which realized the press coverage of the cyber vandalism had generated far more publicity than the studio could have paid for. In a press release, executives noted, "We don't approve of their trashing our Web site, but we are thoroughly impressed by their creativity and ingenuity."[6]

Critics were not particularly enthralled with the film, however. Ryan Gilby of the *Independent* commented, "The loud, silly new adventure *Hackers* . . . can't decide whether its band of avenging computer wizards are the new subversives or the new Peeping Toms."[7] Nevertheless, two of the characters made an impression on at least some critics. Harper Barnes of the *St. Louis Post-Dispatch* noted that Jonny Lee Miller and Angelina Jolie "make an attractive couple, and some of their scenes together transcend the generally unbelievable script."[8]

There was a reason Miller and Jolie crackled together on screen. While filming, Angelina and her co-star fell in love. At least on the surface, Miller seemed like a perfect fit for Jolie. He, too, had come from a family of actors and understood the desire to make a name for himself. He was also just as much of a free spirit, willing to push the edge. However, although their romance would be passionate, it would also be tumultuous and, in the end, unworkable.

Although most people would never have known it to hear him in *Hackers*, Jonathan Lee Miller was British and grew up in the middle class neighborhood of Kingston-upon-Thames. His great-great grandfather was an Edwardian music hall performer and his grandfather was the well-known actor Bernard Lee, who is best known to a generation of filmgoers as M in the first 12 James Bond films. Jonny idolized his grandfather, who had a reputation of being a bit of an eccentric.

Jonny's father, Alan Miller, was a former stage actor who worked at the BBC for 20 years, and Jonny had fond memories of watching in the

wings as his father's television shows were filmed. Jonny grew up wanting
to be an actor and was first hired when he was 10 years old for the BBC
miniseries *Mansfield Park*. He had to grow his hair long for the role and
says he was teased mercilessly about it by classmates. Later, he attended
the all-boys Tiffin School. "I liked it," Johnny says, "even though I'm not
in favor of single sex schools. When I was at that school, girls didn't exist,
which is not a healthy attitude. You get guys coming out of school scared
witless."[9]

Because he already knew what he wanted to do with his life, Miller felt
constrained by school and was a mediocre student. He left Tiffin when
he was 16 and got a job at the Hard Rock Cafe in Piccadilly, which he
viewed as a career move. "I wanted to hang around these crazy, different
people, and besides, it was fantastic, hilarious fun." Plus, there was an ad-
ditional perk. "We all got free hamburgers."[10] His high-spirited nature and
youthful exuberance also occasionally got him into minor scrapes with
the police, though nothing serious. If nothing else, his determination to
be an actor kept him on the almost straight and narrow.

Seeking to move himself up, Miller took a job as an usher at the Drury
Lane theatre. Because the work was mostly in the evening, Jonny was able
to go on auditions for TV roles during the day. One of his first jobs was on
the Granada television series *Families*. Of this role, Jonny would later say,
"My only thought was that I did not have to wear this stupid blue uniform
any more and kiss the feet of American tourists. The reality of course is
that you never stop looking over your shoulder wondering if the work is
suddenly going to dry up."[11]

Nevertheless, the television work kept coming, as did offers for theatre
roles. At one point, Jonny was offered a contract to appear in the long-
running, incredibly popular British drama series, *EastEnders*, but turned
it down. To him, the role would only get in the way of his true ambition,
which was to be a film actor like his grandfather. He would finally get his
chance in 1994 when he was cast in *Hackers* and came to Hollywood for
the first time.

Although Miller doesn't describe his relationship with Angelina as
love at first sight, he does say her beauty was hard to resist. While a movie
is filming, love-struck actors can, and do, spend nearly every waking moment with each other, sequestered in their own little world away from
the responsibilities of everyday life. However, once the movie is over, it is
often a struggle to adapt the fairy-tale romance to the real world; for actors, this often means trying to maintain a new, long-distance relationship
as each of them moves home or leaves to work on another film. This was
the case for Angelina and Jonny, but they stuck it out.

"We had a tumultuous affair 'cause we were living on opposite sides of the world," Miller admits. "But true love is something that just creeps up on you. We'd known each other for a year before we got married."[12] Because they both came from acting families, they believed they could handle the pressure of being married to a fellow actor. On March 28, 1996, when Jolie was only 20 and Miller just 22, the couple impulsively decided to get married.

The decision was so sudden that Jonny didn't even meet Angelina's dad, who was away filming *Mission Impossible* with Tom Cruise, until a few weeks after the marriage. "Being nuts about her had something to do with it," Miller would explain in an interview. "But I also had to think it was a great opportunity to explore other worlds and to move and work in Los Angeles with a purpose. Otherwise I might have been asking *what if?* for the rest of my life."[13]

Although they kept the event quiet, holding the ceremony at Los Angeles City Hall with only two witnesses, they weren't exactly low-key and inconspicuous. Jonny was dressed head to toe in black leather and Angelina wore black rubber pants and a shirt with Jonny's name painted in her own blood. Initially, the newlyweds chose to keep their marriage a secret. However, when she was in Europe promoting the overseas opening of *Hackers*, Angelina disclosed the nuptials during a press interview, commenting, "I always fall in love while I'm working on a film. It's such an intense thing. And I've always been at my most impulsive when English men are around. They get to me. And no we didn't have a big white wedding. We had a small black wedding." At the same time, she saw marriage as romantically noble. "There is no bigger deal than signing a piece of paper that commits you to someone forever," she said.[14]

While Miller was more discreet, Jolie displayed what would become her most notorious trait—giving completely uncensored interviews that often left reporters unsure whether she was serious or pulling an elaborate practical joke. After a while, it became clear she wasn't being a prankster; the only way Angelina knew how to communicate was raw, sometimes uncomfortable truth. About the only thing Angelina didn't openly talk about was her new husband, out of respect for his privacy—although she did comment that he had a distinctly wild side. However, she reveled in describing her own fetishes with knives and tattoos, and openly discussed her sexual interest in women and her curiosity with sadomasochism.

Angelina also made no effort to hide her tattoos, which were all symbolic of something she considered important. The design on her butt was based on tribal totems from Borneo; the one on her arm stood for bravery and the one on her shoulder was Death.

There was only one tattoo that Jolie second-guessed. "I dropped my pants in a tattoo parlor in Amsterdam," she told *People*. "I woke up in a waterbed with this funky-looking dragon with a blue tongue on my hip. I realized I made a mistake, so a few months later I got a cross to cover it. When my pants hang low, it looks like I'm wearing a dagger!"[15]

Like Jolie, Miller fancied tattoos, the most noticeable being the snake on the inside of his wrist, which seemed incongruous with his angelic, pin-up idol face. While *Hackers* might not have been a mainstream hit, enough teenagers saw it that Miller became one of the latest flavors of the month, popping up in teen magazines and fan sites on the web. But like his bride, Miller wasn't concerned with commercial approval or teen idol popularity. He was flattered, but his primary objective was making good films.

Prior to the release of *Hackers* in Europe, Miller's star had brightened considerably in Britain due to his riveting performance in *Trainspotting*, which would later become an art-house hit in America. Directed by Dany Boyle, the film offers an unflinching, though frequently funny, look at the lives of five heroin addicts in Scotland. The movie is adapted from Irvine Welsh's cult novel and is designed to shock, not because it's about addicts, but because of the sometimes-exuberant tone. In tenor, the film harkens back to *Drug Store Cowboy*, which also offended those with conservative attitudes because of its depiction of addicts enjoying themselves. Both films remind the public that there is a reason people first become addicted to drugs—at least in the beginning, drugs can be fun and feel good.

In *Trainspotting*, the protagonists blatantly enjoy doing drugs. However, the film also succeeds in showing the desperate lives these young men lead and the ultimate cost of addiction, from incontinence to death from AIDS. The most notorious scene showed an addict dive into a filthy toilet after some opium suppositories. No glamorizing drug use here. The title of the film is a British slang term that literally means to sit and watch trains, but which idiomatically refers to a heroin-induced state of lethargy and apathy.

Those who saw *Trainspotting*, particularly critics, praised the film's bravery and delicate balancing act. However, the film failed to become a mainstream hit, not necessarily because of the difficult subject matter but because of language. Few American ears could keep up with the heavily accented, highly idiomatic machine-gun dialogue. Miller didn't seem to mind, though. He enjoyed being anonymous in Los Angeles, where he could tool around under the radar of local media scrutiny.

In retrospect, it seems that Jolie and Miller's marriage would inevitably be short-lived, since a relationship built on such passionate intensity often consumes itself. However, in the first year of their togetherness, the sexual electricity between them was tangible. Yet for all their erotic passion, they weren't the most romantic of partners.

More than their youth, more than their exhausting sexuality, more than juggling dual careers, there was one obstacle their relationship could not overcome—Jonny was homesick. When Jolie told him she wanted to move to New York, Miller returned to London. For months after his return to England, the couple shrugged off questions about whether or not they were still together. However, 19 months after they were married, they made it official.

"Jonny and I are still crazy about each other, but we have the sense of needing to move on in different directions," she would tell Louis Hobson of the *Calgary Sun* in 1998. But even then, Jolie seemed reluctant to let go. "Jonny and I are divorced but we're still great friends," she insisted to Hobson in a later 1999 interview. "We've literally held each other's hand through this whole ordeal. There's just never been a lack of love between us. I really enjoy talking on the phone and missing him. We love each other but we realize we can't do this marriage thing together at this time." The divorce became final February 3, 1999.

Jolie says being married to Jonny helped her be a better woman, but it also taught her she needed to let some walls down. "I am so self-sufficient that I don't know how to let a man be a man, or how to commit to buying a house together. I could never even be on the same insurance," she said.[16] For years after, regret colored Jolie's discussion of her break-up with Miller and she once called divorcing him the dumbest thing she'd ever done. In the same breath, though, she admitted she didn't dwell on the past. "I was so lucky to have met the most amazing man, who I wanted to marry. It comes down to timing. I think he's the greatest husband a girl could ask for. I'll always love him, we were simply too young."[17]

Her time with Miller was a crash course in life, on both a personal and professional level, and it would offer some lessons she wouldn't fully appreciate until time had given her perspective. Regarding her experience on *Hackers*, Angelina says now, "It taught me a good lesson. I was just starting out, and I think a lot of young actors take themselves so seriously that unless we're crying and screaming, we don't think we're acting. There's something to just being present and being in the moment and having a good time."[18]

There's also something to being a young, talented actress able to transform herself with each role. Although her next few films after *Hackers* wouldn't be remembered for their box office performances or critical response, they would give Jolie the foundation from which she would explode as one of Hollywood's most promising young actresses.

NOTES

1. Andrei Harmsworth, "I Was Sexual at Nursery Age." April 18, 2007, http://www.metro.co.uk/fame/article.html?in_article_id=45770&in_page_id=7.

2. *Hackers* Press Kit, MGM-UA, September 1995.

3. Ibid.

4. Ibid.

5. "Jonny Lee Miller and Angelina Jolie: The Happy Couple," *Empire*, June 1996, http://www.jonnyleemiller.co.uk/angelinajolie.html.

6. MGM Press Release for *Hackers*, http://209.85.141.104/search?q=cache: UNyBClUkShAJ:www.uncle.com/shake.html+We+don%E2%80%99t+approve+ of+their+trashing+our+Web+site,+but+we+are+thoroughly+impressed+by+ their+creativity+and+ingenuity&hl=en&ct=clnk&cd=2&gl=us.

7. Ryan Gilbey, "A Cat with Nine Former Lives," *Independent*, May 2, 1996, http://www.highbeam.com/doc/1P2-4786214.html.

8. Harper Barnes, "Tripping on the Net: Sophomoric Is the Sum of It," *St. Louis Post-Dispatch*, September 15, 1995.

9. Kate Spicer, "Stand and Deliver, It's Jonny Lee Miller," *Minx*, April 1998.

10. Ibid.

11. *Hackers* Press Kit, MGM-UA, September 1995.

12. Jonny Lee Miller, interview by *Just 17*, http://members.tripod.com/~Odessa-X/justl7·html.

13. Ibid.

14. "Jonny Lee Miller and Angelina Jolie: The Happy Couple," *Empire*, June 1996, http://www.jonnyleemiller.co.uk/angelinajolie.html.

15. Cindy Pearlman, "Angelina Jolie Far from Angelic," *Chicago Sun-Times*, April 18, 1999, http://www.highbeam.com/doc/1P2-4489196.html.

16. Deanna Kizis, "Truth and Consequences," *Harper's Bazaar*, November 1999, http://fansites.hollywood.com/~ajolie/int15.html.

17. Christa D'Souza, "Do You Wanna Be in My Gang? Actor Jonny Lee Miller is Mr. Cool," *Daily Telegraph*, March 17, 2000.

18. Christine James, "'Dancing' Queen Angelina Jolie Gets Constructive in *Dancing About Architecture*," http://www.boxoffice.com.

Chapter 3

LEARNING THE CRAFT

Actors often complain that casting directors can't, or won't, see past the last role an actor played and that they cast based on an actor's physical type. The result of this casting approach is that actors quickly become typecast. It's not surprising, then, that Jolie was next cast as Legs Sadovsky, a disenfranchised teen similar to her character in *Hackers*. The role was for *Foxfire*, the 1996 film adaptation of Joyce Carol Oates's novel, *Foxfire: Confessions of a Girl Gang* (Dutton, 1993).

The novel is set in a blue-collar, upstate New York town during the 1950s. The book follows five high-school girls who form a gang dedicated to pride, power, and vengeance. Together, they aim to fight back against a culture denigrates and destroys young women. A press release for the book described the *Foxfire* chronicles as "the secret history of a sisterhood of blood, a haven from a world of lechers and oppressors, marked by a liberating fury that burns too hot to last . . . Above all, it is the story of Legs Sadovsky, with her lean, on-the-edge, icy beauty, whose nerve, muscle, hate, and hurt make her the spark of Foxfire, its guiding spirit, its burning core . . ." It also calls Legs "one of the most vivid and vital heroines in modern fiction."[1]

As so often happens when a book rich in narrative is adapted for the screen, much can get lost in translation. For example, one of the fundamental elements of the book was its setting in 1950s New York, where American minorities of all kinds were socially repressed and where the seeds of a cultural revolution were being quietly nurtured. The filmmakers, however, chose to update the movie, setting it in present-day Portland, Oregon, where the movie was filmed. Although the setting changed, the central premise remained—a group of high-school girls form an alliance against a sexually abusive male teacher. Their group is indelibly changed by a mysterious new girl, Legs Sadovsky, who director Annette Haywood-Carter describes as a female James Dean.

As the movie opens, a sadistic biology teacher, played by John Diehl, torments one of his female students, Rita, because she won't dissect her frog. As punishment, he gives her detention. In the film, it's widely known among students that during detention he sexually molests girls. However, when Rita shows up for her after-school punishment, she's not alone. Instead, she's accompanied by a group of friends, led by Legs, who leave the teacher beaten and bloody. They are subsequently suspended and move into an abandoned house together. There begins their descent into criminality. The movie is reminiscent of an adolescent *Thelma & Louise*, without the wit or depth.

Jolie saw Legs as someone completely in control, despite her loose-cannon exterior. "She was completely who she was in the moment, and that made her unpredictable," she explained to Diane Anderson of *Girlfriends*. "She was not out of control; she was very there. She was the person always ready to step up to bat to take care of things, and sometimes that might be violent."[2]

Having already experienced working on a film that was never released, Jolie admitted she was prepared for *Foxfire* to suffer a similar fate since it might be perceived as having anti-male sentiments. Perhaps if the film had more faithfully presented the emotional punch of the book, there might have been a maelstrom of controversy. Instead, it stumbled into forgettable melodrama despite a solid performance by Jolie and model Jenny Shimizu, who made her screen debut.

Shimizu was discovered in 1993 getting off her motorcycle in front of L.A.'s Club F**k. At the time, she was working as a garage mechanic. Her androgyny made her the first Asian-American supermodel and she became one of the few openly-lesbian fashion queens. She once joked she had been with every fine girl in the world. Calvin Klein chose Shimizu for his hugely successful CK1 campaign and she appeared in magazine ads around the world. She was also selected as Tokyo's highly touted Shiseido model and, at the time *Foxfire* was filmed, was a much sought-after runway model.

Although she claimed her goal was to open her own mechanic shop, Shimizu did not take her modeling success for granted and was grateful for the opportunities it presented her, which included her acting debut in *Foxfire*. "I absolutely loved this project because it felt so right," she said in an interview promoting the film. "You know when you find something and it just feels right? I know that acting is what I want to do . . . and there are so many strong girls in the film. There's a lot of sexual tension, but no sex." Despite being openly gay, Shimizu says she has never really dated lesbians: "all the women I've gone out with are straight."[3]

Enter Angelina Jolie. Perhaps it was inevitable she would bond with Shimizu, if for no other reason than Jenny's passion for tattoos. During the filming of *Foxfire*, Shimizu had five tattoos, including one of a woman straddling a wrench. Where the logo *Snap-on* should go, Jenny had the words *Strap-on* inscribed instead.

Jolie once claimed, "I probably would have married Jenny Shimizu if I hadn't married [Jonny]. I fell in love with her the first second I saw her. Actually, I saw when she was being cast in *Foxfire*, and I thought she had just read for my part. I thought I was going to lose the job. I said to myself, *Oh, my God, that's Legs*. She's great. We had a lot of fun."[4]

Perhaps the comparison of Legs to James Dean was more telling than the director intended, considering Dean's long-rumored bisexuality and Jolie's previously professed curiosity. While the film skirts any direct discussion of Leg's sexual preferences, critics clearly saw a homoerotic dimension to Jolie's character. Despite this, Jolie claimed, "I honestly could never see her in bed with somebody. I didn't want it to be about that. It was about friendship and bonding . . . it wasn't my role to come in and turn them all gay. If they opened up and questioned themselves down the road—which you could imagine—that's what my role was, to open them up."[5]

In her personal life, Jolie found that she was not only attracted to women in the abstract, but in the flesh. Jolie acknowledged she shared an off-screen romance with Jenny, saying, "I'm quite free with my sexuality. I have a sinister sexual side, but there's also a side to me that's soft."[6]

Jolie's admission of an affair with Shimizu was surprising not simply because it involved another woman, but because she was still newly wed to Miller. "I think he's okay with it," she noted in a 1997 interview. "He came to the set of *Foxfire*. He was around when I was figuring things out about myself . . . When I realized that somebody like Jenny could be a deep love for me, he realized it, and he took it very seriously. If anything, he didn't treat it just like some sexy thing."[7]

Unfortunately for the film and the filmmakers, *Foxfire* didn't have nearly the drama of the behind-the-scenes entanglements. Critics mostly gave a collective shrug. Reviewer Martin Wong found that the "winning performances by Hedy Burress and Angelina Jolie and Jenny Shimizu's big-screen debut can't save Foxfire from spinning into self-parody. From its opening scenes to its melodramatic climax, Annette Haywood-Carter's directorial debut savages the sensibilities of the Joyce Carol Oates book from which it was adapted."[8]

Beth Pinkster of *The Dallas Morning News* agreed, and argued that the film failed in a fundamental way: "Things fall apart when Legs gets sent to a juvenile detention center, leading to the inevitable point: Legs hasn't taught them to think for themselves; she's taught them only to listen to her. The girls remain, as ever, loyal followers who respond to the strongest influence of the moment. They seem destined to end up as beaten wives. And that, above all, makes the film practically a criminal act against Ms. Oates' powerful fiction."[9]

For her next film, Jolie would leave behind the edgy worlds of *Hackers* and *Foxfire* and venture into romantic comedy—an even more potentially risky movie genre, as she would discover. Released in 1996, *Love is All There Is* was written and directed by husband-and-wife team Joe Bologna and Renee Taylor, who also starred in the film. According to Taylor, the film was about the struggle of a mother to let go of her son. "My son married his childhood sweetheart when he was twenty-two and very early on I had to come to grips with letting go of him," she revealed. "The movie came out of that, with the idea of two warring families trying to stop the romance."[10]

To tell the story, Bologna and Taylor wrote a modern-day retelling of *Romeo and Juliet* set in the Bronx. The two "warring" families are the Cappamezzas and Malacicis, rival catering clans who clash over the passionate romance between their 16-year-old children, Rosario and Gina, played by Nathaniel Marston and Jolie. In the film, the two teens star in a one-night community playhouse production of *Romeo and Juliet* and fall instantly in love. To the horror of their parents, they clutch each other far longer than the scene calls for when they kiss in the last act. When the two youths sneak off and get married, the drama becomes operatic in tone. The *Los Angeles Times* was brief in its assessment: "Renee Taylor and Joseph Bologna's *Love Is All There Is* keeps saying that love isn't enough when it's their movie that's not enough."[11]

Jolie's acting career was thus a slow climb in the beginning. After *Love Is All There Is*, she next appeared in an obscure, quickly forgotten 1996 effort called *Mojave Moon*. In just under two years, Jolie appeared in four films, none of which qualified as box office hits. Although the majority of her personal reviews had been positive, she had also been taken to task a few times. Nevertheless, she thought it dangerous to read too much into either extreme. "If you have enough people sitting around telling you you're wonderful, then you start believing you're fabulous. Then someone tells you, *You stink* and you believe that, too," she explained.[12]

As she looked forward to her next project, Jolie was quickly realizing the lesson many aspiring actors before her had learned: working steadily does not ensure your personal life will be equally charmed. It was a fact she had first learned from her father and it was something she was beginning to experience herself. She noted fatalistically, "You don't suddenly have this great life and everything's easy." In fact, Jolie declared, "Nothing ever makes your life better."[13]

However, a few good roles could certainly turn a career around.

NOTES

1. Penguin Press Release, 1994, http://www.robtee.com/books/Foxfire_Confessions-of-a-Girl-Gang.htm.

2. Diane Anderson, "'Tis the Season to Be Jolie," *Girlfriends*, December 1997, http://members.fortunecity.com/foxdm/id88.htm.

3. "Jenny Shimizu: From Grease Monkey to Supermodel," *Curve*, September 1996.

4. Anderson, "'Tis the Season to Be Jolie."

5. Ibid.

6. Drew Mackenzie and Ivor Davis, "I'm Both Sinister and Soft," *Woman's Day* (Australia), April 17, 2000, http://zone.ee/daart/ar42.html.

7. Anderson, "'Tis the Season to Be Jolie."

8. Martin Wong, Review of *Foxfire*, A. *Magazine*, September 30, 1996.

9. Beth Pinsker, "*Foxfire* Extinguishes Oates's Novel's Spark," *Dallas Morning News*, August 26, 1996.

10. Anthony Scaduto, "Flash! The Latest Entertainment News and More," *Newsday*, September 4, 1996.

11. Kevin Thomas, "Love Is All There Is: Tale of Young Love Takes Aim at an Older Audience," *Los Angeles Times*, March 28, 1997, http://www.chicagotribune.com/topic/cl-movie970328-5,1,692960.story.

12. Gary Dretzka, "Angelina Jolie Warily Regards Rising Fame," *Chicago Tribune*, September 4, 1996, Tempo, 5.

13. Dretzka, "Angelina Jolie Warily Regards Rising Fame."

Chapter 4

BREAKTHROUGH

There was a time when film actors studiously avoided television projects. That's because for the first few decades of the medium's existence, the only actors who worked in television did so because they couldn't get big screen jobs anymore. Prime time was a depository for cinematic has-beens who did cheesy guest-spots on shows like *Love Boat*, *Fantasy Island*, and *Murder, She Wrote*. However, with the advent of cable channels like HBO and Showtime, which produced high-quality television movies, the stigma of doing small screen projects dissipated. To keep up, the broadcast networks sought to improve the quality of their content with big-budget miniseries and made-for-TV movies. As a result, actors like Halle Berry, Glenn Close, and Holly Hunter now appear on the small screen as much as they do in movies.

Angelina Jolie's first experience in a big-ticket television production was the 1997 CBS miniseries *True Women*, based on the book by Janice Woods Windle. The historical novel spans five decades from the Texas Revolution to the Civil War. It tells the story of Texas women who created homes on the frontier, bore and buried children, and faced daily threats and obstacles that ranged from Comanche Indians to the Ku Klux Klan to Northern soldiers, and who joined the suffragette movement in their spare time.

Windle got the idea for the book through serendipity. When her son Wayne announced his engagement, Windle wanted to give him and her future daughter-in-law a special wedding present so she decided to collect family recipes and put them in a book. To help, Windle's mother produced an old scrapbook of handwritten recipes she had stashed away. Tucked away with the recipes were also stories about the family's history. However, her children expressed more than a little skepticism about some of the larger-than-life tales recorded as family history and folklore. Ten years later, after exhaustive research, *True Women* was published. In the course of her research, Windle discovered that many of the women in her family were intimately involved in the settling of Texas.

The book focuses primarily on three of Windle's ancestors: maternal great-great-grandmother Euphemia Texas Ashby King; paternal great-grandmother Georgia Lawshe Woods; and great-great-aunt Sarah McClure, who helped settle the central Texas towns of San Marcos and Seguin. The miniseries starred Dana Delany as McClure, Annabeth Gish as Euphemia, and Jolie as Georgia. The production was shot on location for seven weeks in Texas. The miniseries had an added element of uniqueness since executive producer Craig Anderson hired Karen Arthur, a female director.

To prepare for their roles, the three leads visited many historical locations and met with 38 of their characters' descendants. They also visited Sarah's Great House at Peach Creek, built in 1838. Windle says the house was where Sam Houston warned that Santa Anna's forces were advancing, and where five thousand women and children were evacuated to the Louisiana border to escape the Mexican army. *True Women* aired in May 1997 and for the most part, critics and viewers responded positively. However, for once, Jolie was upstaged and the lion's share of ink went to Delany.

In her next project, which was also for television, Jolie was again part of a large ensemble cast. But this time, Angelina's performance was singled out and she suddenly found herself generating that all-important industry buzz that is perhaps the single-most important prerequisite for stardom.

The project that caused industry executives to view Jolie with this new appreciation was The Turner Network's riveting 1997 movie, *George Wallace*, in which she played Wallace's controversial wife Cornelia. For someone who was such a seminal and riveting political figure, it is telling how little Americans under 30 know about Wallace.

George Corley Wallace was born on August 25, 1919, just off Main Street in Clio, Alabama. There, he and his three siblings—Gerald, Jack, and Marianne—lived in a cramped four-room "shotgun" house. Like many rural, southern families during the Depression, the Wallaces suffered many hardships. There's little argument that George's later political leanings were shaped by the rural poverty he experienced as a child, as well as his father's open bitterness about the economic conditions in the South. George, Sr. would often tell his son that southerners couldn't be elected to national office because northerners looked down on them.

With his charming charisma, Wallace quickly rose through the political ranks and sealed his legacy as a politician when he made himself a staunch advocate of segregation. Ironically, in his first campaign for governor of Alabama in 1957, Wallace ran as a liberal with the support of the NAACP, the ACLU, and the Jewish population of Alabama. However, when he publicly opposed the Ku Klux Klan, he lost the election. In response, he adopted a different political stance—the separation of whites and blacks. In the apartheid-like social structure of the 1960s South, Wallace's popularity quickly surged. "He sensed discontentment among the people and he intuited that the entire country was waiting to be *Southernized*," says Marshall Frady, author of *Wallace*, the book on which the movie was based. He explained, "Wallace spoke in code to the issue of racial unease; he condemned the controlling powers in Washington that told citizens who to hire and where to send children to school, which was his code for racial antagonism. He alerted America's political management to a submerged continent of discontent that he himself helped activate."[1]

Even those who weren't alive in the 1960s are probably familiar with one of the decade's most significant images—Governor Wallace defiantly blocking the doorway of the University of Alabama Tuscaloosa to the school's first black students. His rise to power and fall from grace made Wallace one of the most controversial political figures in decades and garnered both enraged critics and staunch allies throughout the country.

"Wallace is the Faust of our generation, a tragic hero who sold his soul," says *Wallace* director John Frankenheimer. "He was a fiercely intense and intelligent man in his time. He knew what he wanted, and the fact that he chose wrong is what this picture is about. This film either will or will not speak for itself, and people can offer criticism after they see it. But whether the audience is for or against George Wallace, I guarantee it will be emotionally moved."[2]

For a time, it seemed possible that Wallace might have the backing and political momentum to be elected President. However, on May 15, 1972, while he was campaigning for the presidential nomination, Wallace was shot five times by Arthur Bremer, a self-proclaimed assassin who had also stalked Richard Nixon and George McGovern. Although he miraculously survived, the shooting caused severe damage to Wallace's spinal cord and left him partially paralyzed, unable to walk, and in constant pain.

The assassination attempt prompted a drastic change in Wallace. According to biographer Frady, Wallace was engulfed in "a misery of spirit" after he was shot.[3] In particular, he was burdened by the assassinations of Martin Luther King, Jr., John F. Kennedy, and Robert Kennedy because he had lived while they had not. Indeed, Frady records that Wallace tearfully apologized for surviving when King's father visited him, and also begged for forgiveness from King's former Montgomery church. "I don't know if he mellowed as much as dimmed; his fierce edge had simply dulled," Frady notes. "The ironic thing, of course, is that if he were never shot, this spiritual transformation, this remorse, probably never would have happened." Frady acknowledges that there is some question about the sincerity of Wallace's regret, but he argues that one shouldn't "quarrel with reforms of the heart, no matter what the foxhole is."[4] Oddly enough, though he never completely regained his political powerbase, Wallace made a remarkable comeback and served two more terms as Governor of Alabama. Most intriguing is that a substantial portion of the state's black voters voted for him.

George Wallace's executive producer Mark Carliner calls the story an epic human tragedy. "It deals with three significant contemporary themes of American society: race and racism; the fundamental danger of democracy; and forgiveness and redemption."[5]

Because of the inherent drama and complex personal relationships Wallace had in his life, casting was particularly critical. The actor who played Wallace would have to cover a span of 20 years and make him both believable and human. Frankenheimer offered the part to stage and screen actor Gary Sinise, best-known now for his work in *CSI: New York*. Also critical was the casting of Wallace's two wives, Lurleen and Cornelia, played by Mare Winningham and Jolie, respectively. "Lurleen was the dutiful politician's wife who sacrificed her health when he ran for governor," says Mare Winningham about Wallace's first wife, who died of cancer. "She would have done anything for her husband, and she ended up giving him her life."[6] After Lurleen died, Wallace married Cornelia, the niece of his political mentor, Big Jim Folsom. Angelina sees Cornelia as "a fiery Southern woman who matched Wallace's energy. She was attracted to his confidence and passion. I think she always loved him and would have stayed with him, but he eventually forced her out," Jolie says.[7]

Director Frankenheimer, who called Angelina "a director's dream," noted that "she brought out the bimboish side of Cornelia, the opportunist, the vulnerability, the sorrow. You saw the loss."[8] Frankenheimer added, "The world is full of beautiful girls. But they're not Angelina Jolie. She's fun, honest, intelligent, gorgeous and divinely talented. She brings a hell of a lot to the party."[9]

George Wallace was unique for a cable movie. It was shot on location in Los Angeles instead of in Canada or another state with lower production costs. The filmmakers had planned to shoot some of the film in Alabama, but then-governor Forrest "Fob" James informed Frankenheimer that the production was not welcome. James later publicly announced, "I wish the scoundrels who are producing this fanciful work of fiction would stay out of this state. They are not fit to trod on Alabama soil."[10]

Frankenheimer begged to differ. "They want us to whitewash George Wallace. We're showing a part of Alabama history. It has our respect—but we're not a documentary, we're a drama. It's a drama based on real events. I think people of Alabama will love this movie. It's important. Racism is still a strong issue in this country. That's why this picture is so important. There's a whole generation that doesn't even know about George Wallace—there are people working on this picture who don't even know George Wallace."[11]

People critic Terry Kelleher took the screenwriters to task for creating a composite fictional black character who works for Wallace but had only glowing words for Jolie. "As for the temperature of Wallace's private life, it soars after his first wife, Lurleen (Mare Winningham), dies and the younger, sexier Cornelia (Angelina Jolie) becomes Alabama's first lady."[12]

Newday's Liz Smith concurred, describing the intimate scenes between Jolie and Sinise as "emotional, intense and magnificently performed."[13]

A lot of people in Hollywood agreed. In 1998, Jolie was nominated for an Emmy for Outstanding Supporting Actress in a Miniseries or a Movie, although she would lose out to Ellen Barkin for her performance in *Before Women Had Wings*. Angelina's breakthrough evening was at the 55th Golden Globe Awards, where she won for Best Performance by an Actress in a Supporting Role in a Series, Mini-Series or Motion Picture Made for TV.

While the Emmys and Academy Awards are arguably the two awards most coveted by those in the television and film industries, respectively, the Golden Globes have earned their own cachet over the years, despite remaining somewhat controversial. The fact that the awards are determined by a handful of foreign "journalists," many of whom are reporters in title only, has caused many to view the Golden Globes as a glorified popularity contest. The suspicion among the cynical has long been that if you take enough of the Foreign Press to lunch, you improve your chances of winning dramatically. What truly gives the Golden Globes its current clout is its proximity to the Oscars, its uniqueness in granting both television and film awards, and the fact that it is televised. And the truth is the Hollywood community enjoys attending the Golden Globes because unlike the more formal Oscars and Emmys, the Golden Globes are one big party, start to finish. Guests are wined and dined—emphasis on the *wined*—prior to the award ceremony . . . and during it . . . and after it. They sit at tables with co-stars and friends instead of in auditorium seats so the atmosphere is more informal. Between the convivial mood and the free-flowing liquor, many of the acceptance speeches, particularly those given later in the evening, are more spontaneous and entertaining than those given at the Emmys or Academy Awards.

As could be expected, the 55th annual Golden Globes ceremony was a celebrity-studded event. In the Grand Ballroom of the Beverly Hilton Hotel, stars from the big and small screens were ushered to their seats. Among those in attendance were *Titanic* stars Leonardo DiCaprio and Kate Winslet; Matt Damon, nominated for both writing and acting in *Good Will Hunting*; Helen Hunt, who had earned Best Actress nods for both her series *Mad About You* and the film *As Good As It Gets*; as well as Steven Spielberg, Jim Carrey, David Duchovny, Gillian Anderson, Jada Pickett, and the casts of *ER* and *Friends*. Also on hand were notable presenters such as Madonna, Goldie Hawn, and Mel Gibson. Jolie was also selected as a presenter in a nod to her second-generation status.

After acting as a presenter, Jolie was again invited to the podium, this time to accept an award. Jolie looked genuinely surprised and just a little flustered. After saying some general words of thanks, she looked down at the statue and then scanned the audience. "Dad, where are you? I love you," she said before walking off.[14] Later on, more than a few people in the audience would comment on the tattoo clearly visible on her shoulder, which prompted her to remark, "If a director doesn't want me because he can't see past my tattoos, I don't want to work with him." Mostly, though, Jolie just felt as if she were having an out-of-body experience. "I was totally in shock. It's like I crashed a party and someone gave me the OK to stay."[15]

After the televised award ceremony was over, the guests mingled with reporters and each other. Jon Voight was beaming when he noted, "Angelina has evidenced such mastery of acting. She has great desire to do good work and will power, so when we talk, I'm mostly just amazed that she knows as much as she does. It's really more a sharing of information and I love hearing her unique approach to things. It's always wonderful when I speak with a real artist. As a father, of course, I'm especially delighted and moved."[16]

Jolie was also moved, but more so by the free-wheeling tone of the evening. "I got really drunk," she told Conan O'Brian when she appeared on his late night talk show. "My dad was with me and so, in the beginning of the night he was really proud of me and then after I started downing tequila he was like, *Oh, do you think that's a good idea?* and then he left."[17]

While her post-ceremony antics might have added to Jolie's personal reputation as wild and free, the award served notice that Angelina was much more than simply Jon Voight's daughter or another pretty face. She was wild, free, *and* extremely talented.

NOTES

1. *George Wallace* production notes, http://alt.tnt.tv/movies/tntoriginals/wallace/prod.credits.notes.html.

2. Ibid.

3. Ibid.

4. Bob Ivry, "A Man and His Times," *Record*, August 24, 1997.

5. *George Wallace* production notes.

6. Ibid.

7. Ibid.

8. Ibid.

9. "Angelina Jolie Biography," *People.com*, http://www.people.com/people/angelina_jolie/biography.

10. Army Archerd, "*Wallace* Exiled from Alabama," *Variety*, January 17, 1997, http://www.variety.com/article/VR1117863009.html?categoryid=2&cs=1.

11. Ibid.

12. Terry Kelleher, "Picks and Pans: Tube," *People*, August 25, 1997.

13. Liz Smith, "The New Courtney," *Newsday*, August 24, 1997.

14. Angelina Jolie, *Golden Globe Awards*, NBC, January 18, 1998.

15. Elizabeth Snead, "*Gia* Taps Angelina Jolie's Wild Side," *USA Today*, January 29, 1998, http://members.tripod.com/~GiaLegs/interviews.html.

16. As heard by Kathleen Tracy, *Golden Globe Awards*, 1998.

17. Angelina Jolie, interview by Conan O'Brien, *Late Night with Conan O'Brien*, NBC, January 29, 1998.

Chapter 5

THE SPLASH

Unfortunately, there are few layered, interesting film roles for women, especially young actresses in the early phase of their careers. As more female filmmakers nudge their way into the business, there seems to be an effort to correct this, but the very nature of the film business makes change difficult. In part, this is due to the enormous amount of money it costs to make a feature with a major studio. Producers often try to hedge their bets by making films that will sell well internationally, such as action adventure movies, or make films that have hugely bankable stars like Tom Cruise or Harrison Ford.

Consequently, for television actors hoping to make the jump to the big screen, a role in a modestly budgeted, independent film is a safer (and more available) choice. There is less pressure and if a small film bombs, the residual effects are far less widespread than when a highly touted, big-budget feature dies a quick and gruesome box office death.

In 1997, few television actors were more popular than *X-Files* star David Duchovny, who presented himself as the anti-star—an actor who openly disdained the trappings of television celebrity. However, Duchovny wasn't against trying to use his small-screen stature to graduate to a big-screen career. Although plans had already been finalized for Gillian Anderson and Duchovny to star in an *X-Files* feature film, 1997's *Playing God* was Duchovny's first opportunity to capitalize on his small-screen success as Fox Mulder. However, almost from the beginning, problems arose that didn't bode well for cinematic success. Two weeks prior to the start of production, the film's original distributor, Columbia Pictures, backed out, citing "creative differences" with the film's production company. Even though Touchstone stepped in and picked up the film's distribution, the experience was still unsettling to Duchovny, who commented that "it's disturbing because you go, *Have I signed on to do a project that sucks?*"[1]

Unfortunately, once the movie was screened for critics, it became apparent that Duchovny's question wasn't as much rhetorical as it was prophetic. In the film, Duchovny plays Dr. Eugene Sands, a drug-addicted surgeon who loses his license when a patient dies on the operating table while Sands is high on amphetamines. After losing his license, Sands becomes the on-call physician for a crime organization run by a mobster named Ray Blossom in order to pay for his drug habit. He also falls in love with the head mobster's girlfriend, Claire, played by Jolie. He eventually has a moral epiphany that leads to a predictable ending.

This ending was a sore spot for Duchovny, who complained, "In the end, my character's redeemed because it's a Hollywood movie. I didn't want to redeem him, but there were other people involved."[2] Despite his unhappiness, Duchovny diligently worked the television talk show circuit to promote *Playing God*. Even so, his agitation showed when he was asked on NBC's *Today* show about the difficulties of transforming himself from a television star to a film actor. "If Robert De Niro had started in *Charles in Charge*, he still would have had the career he had," Duchovny retorted. "I think it is just fate."[3]

For Jolie, the film was a pleasant diversion, in part because it was a more grown-up role than she'd previously had. She describes the experience as "very rock 'n' roll and fun and loud and say-what-you-want-to-say, dress wild and love wild. I really allowed myself to get into that world. Being the age I am, I sometimes feel like a punk kid walking onto certain sets, but I didn't this time. I felt very much a woman."[4]

Working on the film was also enjoyable, in part, because it was better-funded than some of her previous projects. "On a lot of the independent films I've been on, it's been so difficult to pull things together," she told Gary Dretzka of the *Chicago Tribune*. "You're really rushed for time, and there's only one change of wardrobe. You have to be careful not to get a stain on it."[5] During *Playing God*, all Angelina had to do was stay out of the critics' line of fire; however, she managed to do much more, adding to her reputation as a quickly rising star. The film's co-producer, Melanie Green, was Jolie's biggest fan. "She's very beautiful and everybody will be clamoring for her. She has the wisdom of an old soul . . . the grace and style of an older woman. You want to peel away the layers when you meet her."[6]

That said, Green admitted Jolie hadn't been a lock for the role. "In the beginning we thought Angelina was too young . . . Angelina was the last person we saw on the last day of auditions, and she was just awesome," Green said.[7]

Jolie's character was the object of sexual desire for both Sands and Blossom. While sex scenes between Jolie's character and both Sands and Blossom were filmed, neither made it into the final cut. "I think they felt like they couldn't have one without the other so they cut them both," Jolie noted. "It was nice working with [David]. I hadn't seen *X-Files* when I worked with him so I guess that was good. He was very sweet."[8]

She would later comment to *Movieline* writer Michael Angeli, "My gut feeling was they cut the Tim sex scene because they decided they wanted to make a clean, action-type film. I thought it should've been about two people who change each other, like *Pretty Woman*. People love the idea of changing each other, don't they?"[9]

During and after the filming of *Playing God*, Jolie was romantically linked with Timothy Hutton, although both actors' representatives maintained they were simply good friends.

As evidenced from *Playing God's* abysmal box-office showing—it grossed a paltry $1.9 million—it wouldn't have mattered to viewers if the film had ended with a cash giveaway. Critics outdid themselves looking for colorful ways to describe just how poorly the film fared.

Newsday's Jack Matthews mused, "Normally, when the star of a hit TV series is tested with the lead role in a major studio movie, film critics raise their noses and wonder, *Can he make the leap?* In the case of David Duchovny . . . it's more a question of whether he can survive the crash."[10]

Duchovny took most of the critical heat, while Jolie escaped cleanly. *Dallas Morning News* reviewer Philip Wuntch said, "Mr. Duchovny's brooding presence on the home screen has a tendency to seem like mere moping on the big screen . . . Ms. Jolie, who bears strong facial resemblance to her father, Jon Voight, brings presence to the stereotype of a baby-faced tart with a heart."[11]

Michael Medved wrote in the *New York Post* that "Hutton tears into the role with such captivating glee that he may launch an entirely new career for himself playing quirky bad guys. And speaking of launched careers, 21-year-old Angelina Jolie (daughter of screen legend Jon Voight) makes a knockout impression as Hutton's languid, leggy mistress; with her lavishly luxuriant lips, shiny, brittle (and broken) surface, she's nearly perfect as a wounded neo-noir heroine."[12]

Somehow, Jolie had managed to co-star in a bomb and walk away unscathed. In fact, if anything, her stock had risen by her acting sleight of hand. The last time anyone would connect her with the dismal showing of *Playing God* was when she showed up for a special screening of the film. Because Duchovny's mom refused to pay to see the movie, he rented out a movie theater in New York's Time Square. Joining David, his mom, his sister, and his first acting coach, Marsha Halfrecht, were Timothy Hutton and Jolie. Later, they all went out to a bar and celebrated, and then Jolie left and never looked back.

With her personal star rising, it was inevitable that people would wonder if she would ever be professionally paired with her dad. Voight seemed to embrace the idea. "We've thought about it," Jolie acknowledged during an *Empire* magazine interview, adding, "but it would depend on the situation. I know he loves to direct, but for anyone who has the possibility of their father directing them, the rebel that was in them when they were 13 would just come out, the *I'm not going to listen to you!* attitude."[13]

Of more immediate concern to Jolie was the quality of roles being offered to her. "I seem to be getting a lot of things pushed my way that are strong women, but the wrong type of strong women," she commented. "It's like people see *Hackers* and they send me offers to play tough women with guns, the kind who wear no bra and a little tank top. I'd like to play strong women who are also very feminine," such as her character in *Hell's Kitchen*, who Jolie described as "very tough, but . . . also very soft. She ends up pregnant and happy."[14]

Besides Jolie, *Hell's Kitchen* starred Rosanna Arquette as Jolie's mother, and Mekhi Phifer as a troubled youth named Johnny. During a robbery, one of Johnny's accomplices, who is the brother of his girlfriend Gloria, is killed. Johnny is caught and sent to prison, where he learns to box. When he's released from jail five years later, he is determined to turn his life around by pursuing a career in the ring. However, his efforts to start a new life are thwarted by Gloria, who blames Johnny for her brother's death. Before he can move forward, Johnny must confront his past and clear his name.

Once again, Jolie rose above the material. Ernest Hardy of the *New York Times* enthused, "With those impossibly sexy lips, stunning body and a screen-flooding presence, she drags all eyes onto her. More incredibly, though, she delivers as an actress once she's grabbed your attention. And she gives *Hell's Kitchen*—an interesting misfire of a film—a weight and center that it doesn't always deserve."[15]

It almost seemed as if Angelina was biding her time, patiently harnessing her skills until she found the right project in which to unleash her talents. Finally, in 1998, Jolie found the role that would prove to be the perfect complement of material and actress.

GIA

Jolie's slender frame was perfect for her next project, HBO's controversial film *Gia*. Based on a screenplay by Pulitzer Prize-winning playwright Michael Cristofer, the cable film would stretch the boundaries of small-screen drama and put Jolie's stunning performance on center stage. If there was ever a role that seemed written specifically for Jolie, this was it. Indeed, in some ways, one could suspect that Jolie and the real Gia, who is considered one of the first supermodels, were spiritual soul mates—except Jolie learned to overcome her demons in a decidedly less self-destructive a way.

Gia Marie Carangi was born on January 30, 1960 in Philadelphia, and was the daughter of a South Philadelphia hoagie shop owner. When she was 11, her mother Kathleen walked out on the marriage, leaving Gia and her two brothers to be raised by their father. Although Gia and her mother would reestablish a relationship a few years later, the sense of abandonment Gia suffered when her mother left would be an emotionally motivating force for the rest of her life.

As a teenager, Gia began modeling almost by accident. She had modeled a few times in Philadelphia and had done some work for Gimbels. When she was 17, Gia was out dancing at a mostly gay club called DCA when stylist and would-be photographer Maurice Tannenbaum asked if he could take some pictures of her. At the photography shoot, Gia met a woman who knew Wilhelmina Cooper, a former fashion model who owned one of the world's top modeling agencies. The woman took Gia to New York to meet Wilhelmina, where Gia announced herself by carving her name in the receptionist's desk with a switchblade. Despite this, Wilhelmina offered Gia a contract after only 15 minutes.

Gia returned to Philadelphia and mulled over the offer. Her mother supported the idea, spurred perhaps by the fact that she herself had dreamed of being a model when she was younger. Her father, however, had reservations. Gia suspected this was because he didn't like that the modeling agency wanted her to give up her last name and just go by Gia. In the end, she signed the contract and moved to Manhattan.

Despite her self-confidence, New York was still a bit intimidating. "I was scared of the city," Gia once admitted, "because it seemed so huge compared to Philadelphia. And there was a lot of snow, and I had to take a lot of taxis, and I didn't know how to hail them, and I didn't know my way around, and it was really kind of freaky."[16]

At that time, most models were the blonde-haired, blue-eyed patrician beauties like Christie Brinkley. Gia gave the fashion world a darker alternative and soon she was appearing on the covers of *Cosmopolitan* and *Vogue*. By the time she landed her first major advertisement for Gianni Versace, she was earning $100,000 a year. She was 18 years old. By 1980, after she had become the top girl at Wilhelmina Models in New York, she earned five times that much.

Besides her dark coloring, Gia was also a desirable model because of the way she was able to change her appearance, from sophisticated to streetwise to ingénue. Away from the fashion shoots, Gia preferred black leather motorcycle jackets and men's clothing from vintage clothing stores. Everyone in the fashion industry believed Gia had the qualities necessary for a long, successful career.

Not only did Gia have one of New York's most sought-after faces, she also had one of its most sought after bodies. Yet while Gia occasionally slept with men, she was an unapologetic, open lesbian. She frequently made passes at other models, especially when they shared hotel rooms or were on location shoots. In real life, Gia had two great female loves, which were melded into a single composite character in the HBO movie. "She was always that way," comments Jolie, who had access to Gia's journals. "When she was about 13 her mother found letters she had written to girls in school."[17]

Being a top model meant that Gia was welcome at any club. Before long, she was immersed in New York's glittery night life with its endless supply of drugs. At one point or another, she tried everything—pills, coke, booze—but her ultimate chemical of choice became heroin.

At first, her erratic behavior like canceling a shoot because she wasn't in the mood, complaining about the bright lights, or being chronically late for morning sessions, was assumed to be typical bouts of fashion model temperament. However, one particular incident in late 1979 seems very telling in retrospect. Gia canceled a full two weeks' worth of bookings because she said she didn't like the way her hair was cut. She holed herself up in her apartment and refused to come out until it had grown sufficiently. What was excused at the time as eccentric behavior was the first sign of her escalating drug abuse. At other times, however, she seemed completely rational and intuitive. She once noted that when her modeling days were over, "I want a job where I can be out of the limelight making things happen, possibly cinematography. Modeling is a short gig—unless you want to be jumping out of washing machines when you're thirty!"[18]

By 1982, when Gia had been on top of the modeling world for four years, her outlook was more world-weary. Although she was only 22, she felt as if she were "going on eighty four," and had learned success came with a price. "Models are never supposed to be down or be tired or have a headache. They've got to be UP all the time!"[19]

Gia went on to voice a demon that would continue to haunt her—wanting to be appreciated for more than just her physical beauty. "You know, I thank God that I'm good looking or that people think I am good looking. But there's a lot more to it than makeup and prettiness and all that stuff. There's a lot more to being a woman than that. When I look in the mirror, I just want to like myself, that's all. And if I like myself, then I look good."[20]

But the reality was that fashion models were required to maintain a certain physical appearance. In order to maintain her weight at 120 pounds on her 5' 8" frame, Gia mostly survived on fruits and nuts, with periodic juice fasts. Also, as time passed, drugs gained a greater and greater hold over her. Wilhelmina's death in 1980 from lung cancer was a loss from which Gia never emotionally recovered. Former-model Janice Dickinson who worked with Gia recalls, "Gia showed up two hours late for a shoot. Then it took the makeup artist three hours to make her look decent. And then she passed out face down and ruined her makeup. Gia was always doing things like that. We were all just so naughty then."[21]

As her drug addiction accelerated, Gia's behavior became not just erratic but violent, causing her, for example, "to jump through a car windshield when she found one of her female lovers with a man."[22] Gia also had a long fascination with knives and would burnish her blades at anyone she felt slighted her.[23] Her arms and hands were covered by the telltale needle marks and open sores of a junkie. Famed photographer Francesco Scavullo, one of her first mentors, continued to hire her, hoping the work would somehow turn Gia around. It didn't, though, and Gia's career flamed out. Her April 1982 *Cosmopolitan* cover was her last. Gia would later find work selling jeans in a Pennsylvania shopping mall. Although she eventually kicked her habit, her body was failing. In 1986, after being blackballed from modeling, living in a welfare hotel, and getting mugged and raped, Gia was diagnosed with AIDS, contracted through her IV drug-use. Gia died November 18, 1986, at 10:00 in the morning, one of the first women in America to die of complications from AIDS.

It was now up to Angelina to bring her back to life.

NOTES

1. Rebecca Ascher-Walsh, et al., "Fall Movie Preview: October," *Entertainment Weekly*, August 22, 1997.

2. Ibid.

3. David Duchovny, *Today*, NBC, October 23, 1997.

4. Angelina Jolie, "Angelina Jolie," interview by Jon Voight, *Interview*, June 1997, http://www.highbeam.com/doc/1G1-19661469.html.

5. Gary Dretzka, "Angelina Jolie Warily Regards Rising Fame," *Chicago Tribune*, September 4, 1996, Tempo, 5.

6. Ibid.

7. Ibid.

8. Diane Anderson, "'Tis the Season to Be Jolie," *Girlfriends*, December 1997, http://members.fortunecity.com/foxdm/id88.htm.

9. Michael Angeli, "Tres Jolie," *Movieline*, February 1999. http://members.fortunecity.com/jamralla/angel/MovielineFeb99.htm.

10. Jack Mathews, "Don't Quit Your Day Job, David," *Newsday*, October 17, 1997.

11. Philip Wuntch, "PLAYING GOD: Director's Omnipotence Smothers This Thriller," *The Dallas Morning News*, October 17, 1997, 1C.

12. Michael Medved, "Playing God," *New York Post*, http://members.tripod.com/~GiaLegs/articles-pgod.html.

13. "Jonny Lee Miller and Angelina Jolie: The Happy Couple," *Empire*, June 1996, http://www.jonnyleemiller.co.uk/angelinajolie.html.

14. Ibid.

15. Ernest Hardy, "*Hell's Kitchen*: No Escape from the Past, Especially a Criminal One." *New York Times*, December 3, 1999.

16. "50 Most Beautiful People," *People*, 1998.

17. Michael Kilian, "HBO Presents Wild, Sad Story Of Supermodel Gia Carangi," *Chicago Tribune*, January 26, 1998.

18. Mimi Avins, "A Sleeping Beauty: Gia Carangi Had It All, Or So It Seemed in the *Cosmo* Cover Photos of Her," *Los Angeles Times*, January 29, 1998.

19. Francesco Scavullo, *Scavullo Women* (New York: Harper and Row, 1982), http://gia-carangi.home.comcast.net/~gia-carangi/art5.html.

20. Ibid.

21. Mimi Avins, "A Sleeping Beauty."

22. Alanna Nash, "The Model Who Invented Heroine Chic." *New York Times*, September 7, 1997, http://query.nytimes.com/gst/fullpage.html?res=950CEEDB1331F934A3575AC0A961958260&sec=&spon=&pagewanted=all.

23. Nash, "The Model Who Invented Heroine Chic."

Angelina Jolie plays the role of Margaret "Legs" Sadovsky in the coming-of-age film Foxfire *(1996). Goldwyn/Photofest.*

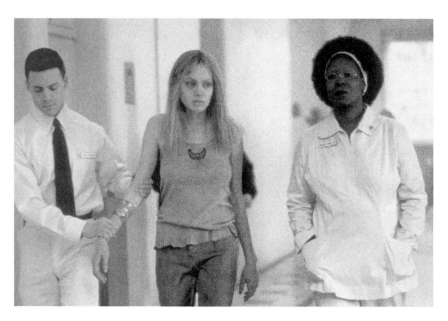

Angelina Jolie's convincing portrayal of a psychiatric patient in the film Girl, Interrupted *(1999) earned her an Academy Award for Best Supporting Actress. Columbia Pictures/Photofest.*

Angelina Jolie, one of the stars of the action film Gone in 60 Seconds, *poses with her then husband, actor Billy Bob Thornton, her father, actor Jon Voight, left, and her brother James Haven Voight at the premiere of the film in Los Angeles in 2000. AP Photo/Chris Pizzello.*

Angelina Jolie (as Lara Croft) in the 2001 blockbuster Lara Croft: Tomb Raider. *Paramount Pictures/ Photofest.*

Angelina Jolie, right, with her daughter Zahara, and Brad Pitt, with Jolie's son Maddox, walk near the Gateway of India, unseen, in Mumbai, India, in 2006. AP Photo.

Angelina Jolie and Brad Pitt make an appearance at the 14th Annual Screen Actors Guild Awards, January 27, 2008. SAG/Photofest.

Chapter 6

A STAR IS BORN

Paramount Studio secured the rights to Stephen Fried's engrossing 1993 biography, *Thing of Beauty: The Tragedy of Supermodel Gia*, shortly after its publication. However, an honest movie about Gia would necessitate depictions of lesbianism, drug use, and violence, and no major studio would touch two of those three issues. In February 1997, HBO announced they would produce their own two-hour movie about Gia, to be written and directed by Pulitzer- and Tony-winning writer Michael Cristofer.

Then-president of HBO Pictures John Matoian felt that HBO movies needed to distinguish themselves from broadcast TV movies. "There's no secret to the fact that we need to be distinctive," he said. "But what I love about Gia is that it's tackling an edgy subject matter that's also slightly more female skewing, which has not necessarily been the traditional HBO audience or movie."[1]

Without question, the movie would live or die on the casting of Gia. When looking over the Hollywood landscape, Cristofer and producer Marvin Worth realized that they not only needed someone with Gia's physicality, but someone with the acting depth to flesh out her character. More than two hundred actresses auditioned, including Jolie. Surprisingly, Angelina wasn't particularly enthusiastic about the prospect of being cast, worried it would "drive me a bit nuts to be that open. I didn't want to do it. I didn't want to go to that place. It was such a heavy story and deals with so many issues. If done wrong, it could have been very bad and not said the right things, and it could have been very exploitive."[2]

What convinced Cristofer to go with Jolie was an essence she shared with Gia. "Angelina is probably as adventurous a person as Gia in many ways, even if she didn't act on all those impulses," Cristofer said with diplomatic understatement. "And she has the quality which I am told Gia had—a pervasive innocence and vulnerability, which I thought was a quality desperately needed. In the hands of the wrong actress, I think Gia could be a person you didn't really want to be in the same room with."[3]

However, Angelina wasn't really sure she wanted to accept the role. "There was a lot of the story that I really identified with, so I didn't want to touch it. Gia was emotionally and literally raped, but she had such a fire for life and in her love for women."[4] In addition, Jolie identified with Gia's struggle to find herself as well as the pain of people not understanding her particular brand of craziness.[5]

But in the end, she accepted the challenge. "Gia has enough similarities to me that I figured this would either be a purge of all my demons, or it was gonna really mess with me," Jolie commented. "I hate heroin because I've been fascinated by it. I'm not immune, but I won't do it now, at all, because luckily I've found something that replaces that high, which is my work. And, probably because I didn't want the part, because I was scared of where it would take me, the producers knew I was right for it."[6]

Jolie's first introduction to Gia was a 1983 *20/20* interview in which an obviously stoned Gia adamantly insisted she was sober. "I hated her," Angelina says. "I didn't believe a word she was saying and it was really hard to watch. Just really sad." However, when she saw some other tapes of Gia, Jolie's opinion softened. "She was talking and being herself, just this regular girl from Philly, and really out there and funny and bold and I fell in love with her," Jolie said. "I think deep down that she was a good person who wanted to be loved. She had a great heart and a great sense of humor and just wanted more excitement."[7]

Also cast in the film were Faye Dunaway as Wilhelmina, Mercedes Ruehl as Gia's mother, and Elizabeth Mitchell as Gia's lover, Linda. Cristofer selected Mitchell over two hundred other actresses after seeing her in Edward Albee's play *Three Tall Women* on Broadway.

While there are still some actors who worry that playing a gay character will somehow negatively affect their career, Mitchell says she thoroughly enjoyed playing Jolie's on-screen lover. "We did this one love scene on the bed where we were laughing so hard we were shaking, the whole bed was shaking," Elizabeth recalls. "The director was yelling, *Stop it, STOP it!*" About Jolie, Mitchell added, "She's all real. She hasn't put herself together at the plastic surgeon's office . . . She's this force of nature. She is a firestorm."[8]

Jolie was equally at ease with the love scenes and commented, "People keep asking, *What was it like to sleep with a woman?* It was fine, it was nice;

she was beautiful. What's the problem?"[9] She downplays a person's outward appearance, saying, "I really don't see anything physical as being that important. I mean, I don't see women, men or black, white. I don't see a handicapped person; I just see the person. I see the aura, the energy."[10]

As Angelina delved more into the character, her understanding of and empathy with Gia deepened. She believes the seminal event in Gia's life was her mother's desertion and that Gia's drug use, her close relationship with Wilhelmina, and even, in part, her attraction to women stemmed from her lifelong desire to fill the void created when her mother walked out the door.

Filming the movie was an emotionally draining experience for Angelina, although in some ways it was also cathartic. "I identified with her a lot," Jolie says. "She's the closest character to me that I've ever played. But in an odd way, playing Gia has made it possible for me not to ever become her . . . I'm able to let it all out and she couldn't."[11]

Co-star Mercedes Ruehl says that during the shoot Angelina's "courtesy . . . was unfailing. She was always on time, always prepared for some heavy emotional stuff. No actor can do take after take like that without some serious technique in her background."[12]

By far, the most difficult scenes in the movie for both Jolie and the crew were those where Gia is dying, with no hair and Kaposi's sarcoma lesions covering her body. In Angelina's mind, it took her impending death for Gia to finally find peace. Stephen Fried, who wrote the biography of Carangi, sees no upbeat end to Gia's life, however. "She isn't a model who just had some problems. This girl did not go back to Oklahoma and live a different kind of life. She died," he emphasized. "Everybody thinks the worst thing that could happen if you send your teenage daughter to New York to be a model is she wouldn't be successful. The worst thing that could happen is what happened to Gia."[13]

Jolie was fresh off her Golden Globe for *George Wallace* when *Gia* premiered on HBO. It was clear that Angelina had arrived. Ed Martin wrote in *USA Today*, "Jolie is dazzling as the doomed beauty . . . Her performance is a remarkably consistent mix of steely strength and crippling vulnerability. Jolie lays bare the real reason for Gia's eventual self-destruction: the exquisite pain of difficult relationships with her self-absorbed mother, Kathleen, and her frequently distant lesbian lover, Linda . . . *Gia* is as hard to resist and as difficult to forget as its stunning title character and the woman who brings her briefly back to life."[14]

Los Angeles Times reviewer Don Heckman was also effusive: "In a role that takes her through a roller coaster of emotions, obsessions and addictions, Jolie is convincing throughout, the kind of performer whose central energy becomes the focus of every scene in which she appears . . . Like the character she is playing, she has the capacity to move past the cant and the artifice into the emotional heart of the drama."[15]

Michele Greppi from the *New York Post* noted, "With all due respect to writers, producers, director and HBO executives, most of the credit for this must go to Angelina Jolie. She fearlessly, even recklessly throws herself into every second. Every movement, every silence, every big, globby tear is a dare to everyone around her to keep up. The result is unforgettable."[16]

In the end, Jolie, who had initially been turned off by Carangi, ended up being seduced by her. "I'd like to date her," she said at the time. "I'd want to be her lover. In her pictures, when she was just hanging out, she had this little half smile, and she looked wild and wicked in a leather jacket. When she's free and just being herself, she's unbelievable; that's the tragedy of her story. You think, *God, she didn't need drugs—she was a drug.*"[17]

FALLOUT

Just as her career seemed ready to explode, Jolie contemplated walking away from it all. Although actors seek out complex, significant roles, there can be a danger in plumbing dark, disturbing emotions. In the months after production of *Gia* wrapped, Angelina found herself adrift. "I was in a place in my life where I had everything I thought you should have to make you happy, and I was feeling emptier than ever," Jolie says. "I was scared of going out like Gia. I needed to just get away and find myself again."[18]

Indicative of her malaise was her take on *Midnight Cowboy*, a film she didn't see until its 25th anniversary screening. "It moves you when you see your parents full of a certain ease and happiness when they were younger," she commented at the time. "I feel I'm past that; I don't feel at ease, that kind of hopeful way of looking at life. To just enjoy life for me is very hard."[19]

Perhaps one reason for her internal struggle was the sense of being compartmentalized by Hollywood and the media. After portraying Gia, a woman who had been labeled by the fashion world, Jolie began to draw comparisons to her own situation and discovered it bothered her. "The thing about this business, they like to stick you in one thing," she observed to Christine James of *Box Office* magazine. "And they like to tell you: *You're the dark person* or *You're the sexy person* or *you're the mother, and you can't be something else.* You just have to keep fighting against it."[20]

She says that while promoting *Gia*, she would go home and consider her relationships, her marriage, and possible motherhood, and wonder if she would ever be a "complete" woman.[21] She believes the source of her turmoil was her work in *Gia*. "I became exposed at the same time that I was playing a role about somebody being exposed. I felt beaten down. I didn't feel like a good person. I felt pretty bad."[22] Adding to her strain was the fact that her work with *Gia* coincided with the end of her marriage to Jonny Miller.

The split from Miller combined with her post-*Gia* malaise threw Jolie completely off course—so much she decided to quit acting, at least temporarily. Jolie moved to London and enrolled at New York University's film school, hoping to reinvent herself and start over. "It was very good for me to get away after *Gia*, to not be in the spotlight, not have a chair. Nobody was getting me a cappuccino in the morning. I was suddenly on the subway with a backpack. Nobody knew me."[23]

Being on her own in New York City was often a scary experience, and after six months of self-imposed exile, Jolie reassessed her situation and came to appreciate what she had left behind. Her epiphany was an emotional crossroads. "I appreciated my career from that moment on. I started opening up again. I started feeling like people weren't a threat to me. I started expressing myself through films as opposed to letting them trap me," she explained.[24]

She realized it was important to actually live life if she wanted to portray it on screen: "I need to learn to relax and not prepare too much, just enjoy life. I notice that my characters go out to dinner and have fun and take these great trips, but I spend so much time on their lives, I don't have much of a personal life of my own. I have to sort of remember to fill out that little notebook on me."[25]

During her time alone, she had also given thought to whether or not she should change her openness with the media. In a lengthy profile by John H. Richardson in *Esquire*, Jolie revealed her father's disapproval at the way she bared her soul in interviews.[26]

However, she didn't take Voight's advice to heart. "I felt like explaining to him that when he was my age, the press was a little different. And you know, he's also not a young woman," she explained, "so he can advise me however he wants, but they'll allow him to talk about things going on in Ireland and the Native American people and his process for his work. They don't ask me those things."[27] Instead, they ask whether she'd ever slept with a woman. She was happy to answer though. "I thought it was nice to share what I had experienced, because I thought it was great," Jolie said. "I didn't see why it was so bad."[28]

Her intent was to share life-lessons learned. "If I choose to talk about something I did when I was 14 years old, and have scars from it, I talk about it because I think I've learned some things from it. And if I choose to talk about a relationship with a woman, I'm talking about it because it's something I've learned about, and it's a beautiful thing. But they just want to sell magazines. And they'll take a quick sound bite and make it a full article, which really does infuriate me, because nobody has learned anything."[29]

Jolie admits that sometimes, though, an actor can be too busy learning. She reveals that she sometimes struggles with letting herself simply be real. She says she sometimes catches herself analyzing other people's emotional reactions instead of just giving them the comfort they need.[30]

But being open is as much a form of therapy for Jolie as it is a promotional facet of her job. And in turn, people have gotten to know a lot about Angelina, which has caused nearly constant speculation about her sex life. The irony of it all, Jolie points out, is that while sexually adventurous she's not been sexually indiscriminate. When she married Jonny Miller, he was only the second man she'd ever slept with. Although she considers herself very sexual, she says she's also monogamous by nature.

If monogamous, she's also uninhibited. The Rolling Stones asked Jolie to appear in their music video for *Anybody Seen My Baby?* In the video, Angelina exposed more than her love of music, undressing for the camera.[31]

Angelina went into her next project with equal abandon. Her New York sabbatical behind her, Jolie returned to work with an outlook that seemed sturdier, more focused, and in some ways, more playful. In the romantic comedy *Playing by Heart*, she played a young woman named Joan who craves love so desperately she arranges to have her car stolen so she can spend more time with her date. Jolie enjoyed showing off her silly side. "Joan is so kooky and crazy, and so different from me. I didn't identify with it, but then I realized I liked it. It made me feel good to do weird things that made people laugh."[32]

She describes her character in *Playing by Heart* as a "very, very extroverted kind of personality who just had no darkness, really, and was just very, very positive, and wanting love. And for me, there is nothing in me that is normally like that or doesn't find that annoying. I had a hard time finding that rhythm in myself. But I eventually found it . . . She's just so hopeful. And I wanted to understand that side of me, and I wanted to answer the challenge."[33]

Playing by Heart brought Jolie more critical praise and many in the media dubbed her as the Next Big Thing. Angelina, however, was careful not to get caught up in the hype. She went out of her way to knock herself off the pedestal. "I'm one of the most flawed people. I woke up this morning and broke the phone by falling over."[34]

Although Jolie was always gracious at premieres and other media events, the heightened attention did create issues with her father. While her father willingly spoke about his daughter at every interview opportunity, Angelina chose not to make that part of her life public.[35] She said relationships with parents change as you get older and it was unhealthy for people to read about her analyzing her father. She emphasized that she cares about her father and appreciates his work, but that her own success should be measured on its own merits.[36]

Buoyed by her sense of professional and personal confidence, Jolie felt ready to take on new challenges and follow wherever they might creatively lead. In the coming year, Jolie's career would crank into even higher gear.

NOTES

1. Army Archerd, "Just for Variety," *Variety*, February 25, 1997.

2. Michael Kilian, "HBO Presents Wild, Sad Story of Supermodel Gia Carangi," *Chicago Tribune*, January 26, 1998.

3. Alanna Nash, "Gia: Fashion Victim," *Entertainment Weekly*, January 16, 1998. http://www.ew.com/ew/article/0,,281498,00.html.

4. Diane Anderson, "'Tis the Season to Be Jolie," *Girlfriends*, December 1997. http://members.fortunecity.com/foxdm/id88.htm.

5. Ibid.

6. Nash, "Gia: Fashion Victim."

7. Ibid.

8. Natasha Stoynoff, "She's Having a Jolie Time Kissing," *Toronto Sun*, June 18, 2000.

9. Elizabeth Snead, "*Gia* Taps Angelina Jolie's Wild Side," *USA Today*, January 29, 1998. http://members.tripod.com/~GiaLegs/interviews.html.

10. Amy Longsdorf, "Angelina Jolie as the Ill-Fated Supermodel in the Biopic *Gia*," *Playboy*, May 2000.

11. Snead, "*Gia* Taps Angelina Jolie's Wild Side."

12. Laurie Sandell, "Reckless Angel," *Biography*, October 1999.

13. Mimi Avins, "A Sleeping Beauty: Gia Carangi Had It All, Or So It Seemed in the *Cosmo* Cover Photos of Her," *Los Angeles Times*, January 29, 1998.

14. Ed Martin, "Gutsy *Gia* Goes beyond Skin Deep," *USA Today*, January 30, 1998.

15. Don Heckman, "Jolie Breathes Life into Gia's Tragic Tale," *Los Angeles Times*, January 31, 1998.

16. Michele Greppi, "Gia: Supermodel in the Raw," *New York Post*, January 31, 1998.

17. Nash, "Gia: Fashion Victim."

18. Longsdorf, "Angelina Jolie as the Ill-Fated Supermodel in the Biopic *Gia*."

19. Bob Heisler, "Talk It Up," *Newsday*, 31 January 1999.

20. "Is Angelina Jolie the It Girl For the 21st Century?," *Jezebel*, February 2000. http://angelanna3.tripod.com/interviews2000/id9.html.

21. Mimi Udovitch, "The Devil in Miss Jolie," *Rolling Stone*, August 19, 1999. http://www.rollingstone.com/news/story/5939518/the_devil_in_miss_jolie.

22. Trish Deitch Rohrer, "Dangerous Beauties: Winona Ryder and Angelina Jolie Walk on the Wild Side," *Premiere*, October 1999.

23. Andrew Essex, "Girl Uncorrupted: Razor-Sharp Turns in *Gia* and *Wallace* Got Her Noticed," *Entertainment Weekly*, November 5, 1999.

24. Longsdorf, "Angelina Jolie as the Ill-Fated Supermodel in the Biopic *Gia*."

25. Michael Angeli, "Tres Jolie," *Movieline*, February 1999, http://members.fortunecity.com/jamralla/angel/MovielineFeb99.htm.

26. John H. Richardson, "Angelina Jolie and the Torture of Fame," *Esquire*, February 2000.

27. James Kaplan, "Holy Moly. It's Angelina Jolie," *Allure*, March 1999.

28. Richardson, "Angelina Jolie and the Torture of Fame."

29. Kaplan, "Holy Moly."

30. Angeli, "Tres Jolie."

31. Angelina Jolie, interview by Conan O'Brien, *Late Night with Conan O'Brien*, NBC, January 13, 2000. http://www.geocities.com/angelina_jolie_fan_page/talkshow980129.htm.

32. Jack Garner, "Jolie's Performance in *Playing by Heart* Is Drawing Attention," *Gannett News Service*, January 21, 1999.

33. Ibid.

34. Longsdorf, "Angelina Jolie as the Ill-Fated Supermodel in the Biopic *Gia*."

35. Deanna Kizis, "What the Hell Is Wrong with Angelina Jolie?," *Jane*, February 2000.

36. Bob Ivry, "A Man and His Times," *Record*, August 24, 1997.

Chapter 7

FINDING HER CENTER

In January 1999, Angelina Jolie shone golden again when she earned her second Golden Globe for her work in *Gia*. Jolie, accompanied to the awards by her soon-to-be ex-husband Jonny Miller and her brother James Haven, promised to do something wild and crazy if she won. Because the event was held at the Beverly Hilton Hotel, she had the perfect idea. As a teenager, Jolie and some of her buddies were kicked out of the hotel for jumping into the pool with their clothes on. So after the ceremony was over, first Miller, then Haven, and finally Jolie dove into the pool. Dripping and smiling wide, Jolie climbed out of the pool and posed happily for photographers in her soggy, hand-beaded Randolph Duke gown.

Jolie says it's the way awards should be celebrated. "To me it's funny that everyone isn't jumping in the pool because it's one of those nights. It's always surprised me that at one of those awards things, where there are wild people, free people, everybody is so serious, tamed by it all," she remarked.[1]

Next on the horizon for Jolie was a film about air traffic controllers that would not only keep her career flying high but also make her personal life soar as well. Like many films, *Pushing Tin* began its life as a magazine article. In 1996, the *New York Times Sunday Magazine* published an article written by Darcy Frey called *Something's Got to Give*. The feature was a behind-the-scenes look at the inner workings of the high-pressure New York Terminal Approach Radar Control (TRACON) center and profiled several of the controllers.

As soon as Hollywood producer Art Linson read the article, he wasted no time optioning the rights to the story. "I read the piece and immediately thought it would be a great premise for a movie," Linson said. "Darcy's article was funny, serious and truly original. He captured the juxtaposition of the dramatic hazards of these guys' jobs with the comic energy of their personal lives and exposed the readers to a strange new world, a world we certainly have never seen on film before."[2]

Linson hired brothers Glen and Les Charles, who wrote and produced *Taxi* and co-created *Cheers*, to collaborate on turning the article into a script, which would become known as *Pushing Tin*. Once the screenplay was completed, Linson and Laura Ziskin, president of Fox 2000 Pictures, offered the script to British director Mike Newell, at that time best-known for *Four Weddings and a Funeral*. At the time, Newell had just finished the intense movie *Donnie Brasco* with Al Pacino and Johnny Depp and was looking forward to taking a break to recoup.

"I was tired," Newell recalls, "and I was by no means sure that I wanted to go back to work. But I took a look at the script, did some work with Glen and Les and fell in love with them. They are two very inventive, receptive and bright men. . . . wonderful writers. I so enjoyed working with them that my involvement in the project sort of rolled on from there."[3]

Newell considers the movie to be "about people crashes, not plane crashes." As Newell describes it, air traffic controllers are "macho, dominant, messianic" men who work in an enormously dangerous environment.[4] The overwhelming responsibilities of air traffic controlling act almost like an infection: "it starts to invade every aspect of their lives, infecting their health, their marriages, and their minds. These guys are obsessed with and terrified by their job at the same time. They have to find all sorts of escape routes in their emotional and psychological lives. The fallout of all this stress is where the drama, the gallows humor and the morality tale come together in the story."[5]

The movie focuses on the rivalry between two hotshot controllers, Nick Falzone and Russell Bell, played by John Cusack and Billy Bob Thornton. While the movie hinges on the conflict between Russell and Nick, director Newell believes the glue that held everything together were the performances by Jolie and Cate Blanchett as the controllers' wives, Mary Bell and Connie Falzone.

Newell describes Angelina as "an extraordinary-looking creature like some weird, undiscovered orchid. She had that little lost bad girl thing which, really, she brought to the part. There really wasn't much there on the page for her character, and she filled in the blanks. She's a brave, bold girl. I kept checking her age thinking, is she really this young to be this good?"[6]

Jolie's character, Mary, who almost breaks up Nick's marriage, is the consummate bad girl. She's sexy, she drinks too much, she sleeps around.

While the character might be intended to be "cool," in Jolie's opinion, she is "pathetic."[7]

At the time, both Jolie and Blanchett were professionally hot. Cate had been nominated for an Oscar for her performance in *Elizabeth* and Jolie had been wracking up awards the previous year for *George Wallace* and *Gia*. Both actresses agreed that the attraction to *Pushing Tin* was in large part due to Newell, who Blanchett describes as a fantastic director who understands how to maintain that blend between humor and pathos.[8]

As Mary Bell, Jolie was pitted on-screen opposite Billy Bob Thornton, whose status within the film community had risen considerably the previous several years. He was nominated for a Best Supporting Actor Oscar in 1999 for his work in *A Simple Plan*. That same year he was also honored with a Los Angeles Film Critics Award and Broadcast Film Critics Award for his supporting performance in *Primary Colors*. However, it was his critically acclaimed 1996 film *Sling Blade*, which he directed and starred in, that put Thornton on the Hollywood map. For his efforts, he was honored with an Oscar for Best Adapted Screenplay and an Academy Award nomination for Best Actor. All the exposure didn't do much for his public image, though. At the time, he commented, "I still think people are staring at me because they're afraid I'm gonna rob them or something! I'll be standing in a coffee line, and someone really staring at me will come up and then ask for my autograph. And I'm like, thank God, you know?"[9]

Pushing Tin opens with the following epigraph: *You land a million planes safely, and then you have one little midair and you never hear the end of it.* The movie intentionally plays out like an updated western. Nick "The Zone" Falzone is the top-gun controller whose confidence is undermined when a new controller from out West, Russell Bell, is hired. Nick and Russell's every encounter becomes a competition that slowly erodes at the foundations of Falzone's life.

The *mano-a-mano* posturing of the script spilled over onto the set, according to Newell. "There was a tremendous amount of top-dog, bottom-dog stuff as to who could do the job best, ad-lib better, get into the shot . . . They were constantly jockeying for position," Newell says. For example, in one scene, the script called for Russell to lose a game of one-on-one basketball to Nick, but when the cameras rolled, all bets were off and Thornton refused to fake a defeat.[10]

For Angelina, the movie was an exercise in enjoyment and her most fun acting experience to date. "I started working on it right after I'd just come out of my dark period," Jolie remarked. "I was really happy on the set. I loved my character and all the people on the set were such fun to be around. I really understand the whole theme of the film, which is dealing with your personal demons and with fear . . . If I hadn't put a few of my demons behind me, I don't think I'd have felt as secure and happy as I did working on *Pushing Tin*."[11]

However skillfully the movie was put together, *Pushing Tin* defied easy classification. It wasn't a straight comedy or a relationship movie or a buddy movie or noir, which is what director Newell said he liked about it. Unfortunately, that was precisely what critics didn't. Despite this, Jolie again demonstrated her Teflon-like coating against negative reviews. "This is the first high-profile movie role for Angelina Jolie," noted *Entertainment Weekly's* Owen Gleiberman. "And already it's clear that she's that rare thing, a sex bomb who is also a major actress. In *Pushing Tin*, Jolie brandishes her bangs, her crooked bee-stung pout, and her tawny ripe body with seductive abandon, yet she also makes Mary a wounded, insidious basket case."[12]

Pushing Tin was criticized by some reviewers for not including some of the more dramatic information from the original magazine article it was based on. Even so, it was a fairly safe bet *Pushing Tin* wasn't going to be a film airlines would show on their flights. Jolie, however, remained un-phased by the subject matter. "I have no fear of flying," she says. "I've always been convinced that I wouldn't die in a plane. That's just not how I'm going out."[13]

By the summer of 1999, Angelina Jolie was not only an actress to be reckoned with, she was suddenly the darling of the magazine world, with her face adorning the covers of publications on a monthly basis. Typically, Jolie downplayed the attention. "You get a couple of big movies so they put you on magazine covers," she said dismissively. "People talk about you and the hype gets back to the studios and they decide they can capitalize on your sudden celebrity. It's doesn't mean I'm a better actress than I was when they didn't want me in their pictures. It just means that people recognize my name and that makes me a viable commodity."[14]

Jolie had once been romantically linked to Timothy Hutton during the filming of *Playing God* and the rumors were re-fueled when Jolie and Hutton were seen together Oscar night 1998 but refused to pose for pictures. Jolie's manager insisted the two had been friends since making the 1997 movie and that they simply hooked up for Miramax's post-Oscar bash at the Polo Lounge. Whatever the truth of their friendship, Jolie hadn't had a truly serious, long-term relationship since she and Miller separated. And often, Angelina seemed to be working out her personal questions every time she gave an interview, which is perhaps why she once observed, "I don't need a therapist. My choice of screen characters is my therapy.

Acting is my way of tapping into different aspects of my own personality. There is a side of me that is intensive. I think that distances some people from me. I need to learn to need other people. I need to let people hug me without tensing up."[15]

Although the relationship would develop slowly and largely out of the public eye, during the making of *Pushing Tin*, Jolie believed she had found a kindred soul in Billy Bob Thornton, who had been divorced four times and who was presumed to be seriously involved with Laura Dern. But instead of rushing headlong into a relationship as she had with Miller, Jolie let life come to her at its own pace. In the meantime, she kept focused on her career, making typical Jolie decisions. In April 1999, it was announced that she would star in *Dancing in the Dark* for Warner Bros. The film was a remake of Cornell Woolrich's suspense novel, *Waltz into Darkness*. Directing would be her *Gia* director Michael Cristofer.

One role Jolie turned down was the remake of *Charlie's Angels*. An erroneous wire service story reported she had joined Drew Barrymore and Cameron Diaz in the cast, and then-Columbia Pictures chairwoman Amy Pascal admitted it was perhaps a bit of wishful thinking, calling Jolie "a female James Dean for our time." Pascal also said, "I'd make any movie with her in it. I begged her to do the film version of *Charlie's Angels*. But she's no angel."[16]

Later, Jolie recalled that when Columbia sent her the *Charlie's Angels* script, they gave her three reasons she should do it. "They said there hadn't been really good, strong roles for women; that it would make me a big star; and that I would have a fun time doing it." She begged to differ. "All my roles so far in *Gia*, *Wallace*, *Playing by Heart* . . . have been strong female roles. The idea of being a big star has absolutely no appeal to me." In fact, she called the notion of doing a big movie simply to become a star was frightening. Plus, she had already agreed to take part in the remake of *Gone in 60 Seconds* with Nicolas Cage. She was happy letting that be her "fun" movie.[17]

Plus, Jolie didn't think she was right for the role, which eventually was played by Lucy Liu, saying that she knew she wouldn't fit or find it fun after reading the script.

Although Jolie did admit that the *Charlie's Angels* script was "cute and clever," she also pointed out that "Drew Barrymore and Cameron Diaz are already celebrities and they're going to have great fun spoofing their images with *Charlie's Angels*. I'm not at that point in my career, so audiences won't have as much fun watching me run around in high heels chasing bad guys and flipping my hair."[18]

Instead, Jolie's next movie would portray a much darker side of life.

NOTES

1. Bob Thompson, "Johnny Be Good: Actor, Writer and Producer Cusack Is Still Learning," *Edmonton Sun*, April 20, 1999.

2. *Pushing Tin* production notes, Fox, April 1999. http://www.cinemareview.com/production.asp?prodid=556.

3. Ibid.

4. Ibid.

5. Ibid.

6. Alison Boleyn, "Celebrity Profile: Angelina Jolie," *Marie Claire*, February 2000. http://angelanna3.tripod.com/interviews2000/id7.html.

7. James Kaplan, "Holy Moly. It's Angelina Jolie," *Allure*, March 1999. http://www.wutheringjolie.com/nuke/modules.php?name=Content&pa=showpage&pid=360.

8. Cate Blanchett, "Pushing Tin," *Evening Standard*, October 26, 1999, http://www.geocities.com/hollywood/Land/9730/tinarticle1.html.

9. Prairie Miller, "A *Simple Plan*: Interview with Billy Bob Thornton," *Star Interviews*, January 1, 1998.

10. Raymond A Edel, "People," *Record*, April 15, 1999.

11. Louis B. Hobson, "Pushing Her Luck: Angelina Jolie's Full-Tilt Existence," *Calgary Sun*, April 18, 1999. http://jam.canoe.ca/Movies/Artists/J/Jolie_Angelina/1999/04/18/759417.html

12. Owen Gleiberman, "Pushing Tin," *Entertainment Weekly*, April 23, 1999. http://www.ew.com/ew/article/0,,64000,00.html.

13. Chuck Arnold, "Chatter," *People*, May 3, 1999, http://www.people.com/people/archive/article/0,,20128100,00.html.

14. Francine Parnes, "The Sweet Face of the Future," *Daily Telegraph*, May 26, 1999.

15. Louis B. Hobson, "Jolie Intense to the Bone," *Calgary Sun*, Oct 31, 1999.

16. Louis B. Hobson, "Angelina Jolie is no Angel," *Ottawa Sun*, August 30, 1999, http://jam.canoe.ca/Movies/Artists/J/Jolie_Angelina/1999/08/30/759416.html.

17. Jeffrey Ressner, "Rebel Without a Pause," *Time*, January 24, 2000, http://www.time.com/time/magazine/article/0,9171,37644,00.html.

18. Hobson, "Angelina Jolie is no Angel."

Chapter 8

ABOVE THE TITLE

On more than one occasion, Angelina Jolie has admitted to liking "dark things." As a result, one could expect that she absolutely loved filming *The Bone Collector*, the 1999 film based on the best-selling thriller by Jeffery Deaver. Jolie played Amelia Donaghy, a rookie street cop who teams up with a quadriplegic detective and forensics specialist named Lincoln Rhyme (Denzel Washington). She becomes Rhyme's ears, eyes, and legs, and together they work to catch a vicious serial killer who is causing mayhem on the streets of Manhattan. As they work together to stop the killer, Amelia and Rhyme become drawn to each other both professionally and personally.

Deaver says the detective's physical impairment "explores some of the issues about who we are in the perfect body cult of today's society. And what we are really, in essence, we are our minds. I wanted to create a character that was basically pure mind, an accomplished mind, as worthy and as savvy as the classic, mobile detective."[1]

Director Phillip Noyce says he was drawn to the script because he saw it as four stories in one. "It's a love story. It's a thriller. It's a detective story. And it's a story of renewal and resurrection. Two people have lost themselves and given up, they find each other, and ultimately, the will that had failed them."[2]

Noyce says Jolie possessed the perfect complement of qualities for the role of Amelia Donaghy. "She had to be young, in her mid-twenties, with the strength to play a New York cop, as well as a very special vulnerability," he explained. He says he saw all of those qualities in her *Gia* performance. "The strength and the vulnerability, and also a fearlessness, both in the character she portrayed and—I realized when I met her—as an artist."[3] Washington was also given control over who would be cast as his co-star. After viewing her work, Denzel agreed to meet Angelina to see if they would have the right chemistry. Angelina was thrilled that Denzel was impressed enough with her work to meet her and thought that he would be perfect as Rhyme. "It wasn't just that he's a great actor; I could really see him as this man," she said. "I don't think there are many actors that could be that still and have that kind of presence."[4]

Despite Jolie's budding reputation as one of Hollywood's most talented young actresses, Noyce and producer Martin Bregman had to fight the studio to cast her. "Phillip and Marty had seen me in *Gia* and wanted me for the role," Jolie says. "The studio wanted a bigger-name star. The only way the studio would take me was if Marty cut $20 million off the budget."[5]

Angelina considered the subtle romance between Rhyme and Donaghy magical. "In other movies you'd have dinner date scenes and sex scenes," she says, describing typical screen relationships. Instead, "Denzel and I had days of scenes where I'd have to help him move something or show him something or give him some juice. And when we'd talk we'd have to look at each other. He couldn't hold me . . . so his character was more connected to me sensually. The slightest touch was electric. It doesn't hurt that Denzel's a stunning and intelligent man and a very powerful presence—he is mesmerizing."[6] Indeed, the romance between Amelia and Rhyme was completely believable. In part, this was likely because of Angelina's personal ideas about relationships. "I genuinely see past things like physical deformity, color, race and sex," she explains. "To me attraction is an aura thing. It's an energy given off by the other person that you react to or you don't."[7]

Jolie, who has had only a handful of partners in her life, says that the relationship between Amelia and Rhyme changed her view of relationships. "There are very few people that can hold me; that I can talk to about my life and can make me cry," she says. "There are few people who I'd want to come to and say, *Look at what I did.* I can have sex with anyone, but there's hardly anyone to share things with." Compared to the relationship she developed with Denzel in the film, no purely sexual relationship was sufficient in her eyes. "If they weren't interested in my work and how I was feeling, then it didn't come close to what I was experiencing at work on the set," she explains.[8]

The Bone Collector also offered Denzel a terrific opportunity. "To play a person who is quadriplegic is a great challenge for any actor. An actor's body is his instrument, and to have 93% of that taken away, you have to sort of act with your soul," he said. In the course of preparing for the movie, Denzel discovered the role was even more challenging than he had imagined. In particular, the physical restrictions, like being unable to turn his head or even laugh from the belly, were very difficult for him as an actor.[9]

Ironically, the physical limitations of Washington's character also restricted Jolie on camera. "It subdues your movement when you're with someone who can't move," she explains. "I naturally didn't touch his bed, or move out of his eyeline. You find yourself being stuck."[10]

To prepare for the role, Jolie met with several policewomen and visited an actual forensics lab in New York. She also viewed pictures of crime scenes not far away from where she was living. "I had to do it to know what my reaction would be. You can't swallow, your mouth drops open and you just feel your guts empty. It's not emotional—it's a physical reaction," she says.[11]

Donning a police uniform also helped Angelina get into character. "There is something about the police uniform and especially the gun that makes you stand, walk and talk differently," she remarked. "It gives you such a feeling of authority that you begin gesturing toward the gun when you talk."[12] Jolie says the cop mentality followed her home, too. "One night I was going home and there was an accident on the side of the road. I got out of my car and started moving traffic and thought, *Why aren't they blocking off the crime scene? Why aren't they removing evidence from the other car?*"[13]

The Bone Collector represented a major career milestone for Jolie insofar as it was the first time her name had ever appeared above the title. "I fell over laughing when I found that out," Jolie admitted shortly before the film opened. But she also had some doubts about playing a police officer. It seemed a little frightening for her to play a role like that when in her mind, she looked like she was so young.[14]

This is why she didn't have animosity toward the studio executives who were nervous about casting her. "It took months," she says, for her approval to come through, "I had to basically wait and wait and wait and beg and not take another job. But I don't blame them—I'd certainly never had a moneymaking film. They took a big risk."[15] While Jolie understood about the studio wanting a "bigger name," she was bothered by their concern that she was white and Denzel black. "I heard that and I thought it was a joke," she said of their hesitation.[16]

It is telling that despite the hoops the producer and director had to jump through to hire her, Angelina wasn't tentative about butting creative heads. Her appreciation and gratitude didn't extend so far that she would compromise herself artistically. One area of early contention was that the script called for Amelia to have been a model prior to joining the force. "I fought them on that for awhile," she recalls. "I insisted that the modeling be in high school or college. Then it ended up being funny because she's in Catholic school clothes—so it made it that much more outrageous."[17]

Nor did Jolie think it necessary for her character to have a sex scene early in the movie. Obviously, her objection had nothing to do with nudity in and of itself, as anyone who saw her in *Gia* would know. Jolie does not see nudity as a private thing so she doesn't find disrobing shocking or sexy, but felt it was necessary in *The Bone Collector*. As a result, an early scene that called for her to be nude was eventually discarded.

Jolie also took a stand on her wardrobe in the film's final scene in which she and Washington appear together socially. The filmmakers wanted her to don a little red party dress but Angelina said there was no way Amelia would ever wear such a frock.

Prior to the film's opening, Angelina happened to be driving down Sunset Boulevard in Los Angeles and saw a billboard advertising the film. Seeing a giant-sized photo of herself next to Denzel nearly caused her to have an accident. As the premiere date loomed, the filmmakers and cast hoped that the film did as well as the high-scoring test audiences indicated it would. When the film was screened for a focus group in Paramus, New Jersey, the audience raved about Jolie, prompting Washington to joke, "And what about Denzel? Don't you think *he* was great?"[18]

Critics were less enthused about the film but generally gave the actors good marks. *People* magazine said, "Restricted to acting mostly from the neck up, Washington manages to create a vivid portrait of a complicated man who is alternately depressed, self-mocking and obsessed with his job. The talented Jolie, all sharp edges and attitude, proves a worthy match."[19]

Philip Wunch of *The Dallas Morning News* took issue with what he considered the throwaway bad guy. "It's a nondebatable cinematic fact that a thriller is only as thrilling as its villain. Yet everyone connected with *The Bone Collector* . . . must have forgotten that truism. Denzel Washington is fine, Angelina Jolie is more than fine, and Phillip Noyce's direction is frequently astute. But the film's impact is dulled by the lack of emotional investment in the villain. When the heinous being is finally revealed, you'll shrug and think, *So what?*"[20]

It just goes to show that in the end, negative reviews don't necessarily affect a film's ultimate success because despite lukewarm reviews of the movie itself, *The Bone Collector* was the number one film at the box office the week it opened, earning an estimated $17.2 million and further cementing Jolie's status as someone who could "open" a film. However, it was her next movie that would firmly solidify Angelina as an undisputed member of Hollywood's new royalty.

NOTES

1. William F Nicholson, "'Terrible Lawyer' Keeps Wheels of Justice Turning," *USA Today*, August 13, 1998, 4D.

2. *The Bone Collector* production notes, Universal Studios, November 1999. http://www.thebonecollector.com/crimelab.html.

3. Mimi Udovitch, "The Devil in Miss Jolie," *Rolling Stone*, August 19, 1999, http://www.rollingstone.com/news/story/5939518/the_devil_in_miss_jolie.

4. Sherry Weiner, "Interview with Angelina Jolie," 1999, Univercity.com, http://members.fortunecity.com/ajonline/information/articles/012.htm.

5. Louis B. Hobson, "Dark Angel: Angelina Jolie Has a Decidedly Sinister Side," *Calgary Sun*, November 4, 1999, http://members.fortunecity.com/ajonline/information/articles/022.htm.

6. Weiner, "Interview with Angelina Jolie."

7. *The Bone Collector* production notes.

8. Weiner, "Interview with Angelina Jolie."

9. *The Bone Collector* production notes.

10. Ibid.

11. Weiner, "Interview with Angelina Jolie."

12. Hobson, "Dark Angel."

13. Weiner, "Interview with Angelina Jolie."

14. Bob Thompson, "The Many Faces of Angelina," *Toronto Sun*, April 11, 1999.

15. Andrew Essex, "Girl Uncorrupted: Razor-Sharp Turns in *Gia* and *Wallace* Got Her Noticed," *Entertainment Weekly*, November 5, 1999.

16. Ibid.

17. Weiner, "Interview with Angelina Jolie."

18. Anne Bergman, "A Proverbial Adventurer," *Los Angeles Times*, November 17, 1999.

19. *People Weekly* 52, no. 19 (November 15, 1999): 35.

20. Phillip Wuntch, "*The Bone Collector*: Villain Doesn't Have a Spine," *Dallas Morning News*, May 11, 1999, 1C.

Chapter 9

GIRL, INTERRUPTED

Girl, Interrupted is a project that suffered through what Hollywood insiders call "development hell." Producer Douglas Wick first optioned Susanna Kaysen's book about her incarceration in a mental institution in 1993. A short time later, Winona Ryder was attached to the project as both star and producer, putting it on the production fast-track. But after scripts by three different writers failed to make the cut, *Girl, Interrupted* stalled. Desperate for the project to be resurrected, Ryder approached director James Mangold. "I was unsure about getting involved," he admits. "I thought everyone wanted a Lifetime movie—weepy girls in smocks, all retching and twitching. I said, *I want to make a monster movie*, a movie about what it's like to lose your boundaries in your world."[1]

Prior to the release of the film, Mangold observed that women were done a disservice by many films "because movies geared toward them are all so fuzzy and pastel." Mangold wanted to correct this. "I wanted to bring some of the edge of my other movies to this one, which is, naturally, going to be construed as a *chick flick*. That was the challenge—to give a women's film some *cojones*."[2]

Girl, Interrupted chronicled author Susanna Kaysen's nearly two-year experience in a mental institution. Her incarceration was prompted by a half-hearted suicide attempt in which she washed down a bottle of aspirin with a bottle of vodka. Prior to her suicide attempt, Susanna had been a growing concern to her Boston blueblood parents because of her rebellious behavior, such as nodding off through her high school graduation and her apathy about attending college. After a therapist who was a "family friend" took only 20 minutes to determine the 17- year-old suffered from "borderline personality disorder," Susanna was checked into the McLean Psychiatric Hospital, which is given the fictional name Claymoore in the film. Kaysen's hospitalization took place during 1967–1969; despite the cultural upheaval that rocked so many other parts of American life at that time, mental illness was still a dirty little secret. Schizophrenia, manic depression, anorexia, and bulimia weren't household words yet and a loved one suffering any emotional distress was usually hidden from sight. As Kaysen's memoir shows, insanity can hold an odd comfort. Indeed, Kaysen's major dilemma is convincing herself it is better to heal and rejoin the world than stay cocooned in a place she really doesn't belong.

Because of its themes, *Girl, Interrupted* was often compared to other films of the same ilk. When discussing it, industry insiders referred to the prospective film as *One Flew over the Cuckoo's Nest* meets *Stand by Me*, or *Snake Pit* meets *One Flew over the Cuckoo's Nest*. However, to star Winona Ryder, the film was simply her obsession—partly because she was personally familiar with the territory. Shortly after finishing the film *House of the Spirits* in 1992, Ryder had checked herself into a psychiatric clinic for five days. Although still a teenager, Ryder was already a veteran of a dozen films and was having trouble dealing with the stresses of too much work, too little sleep, and not enough emotional grounding. In addition to the external pressures of work, Ryder was also hurting on a more personal level. She had recently broken up with fiancé Johnny Depp, ending a four-year relationship.

"I was actually in for five days," she says of her clinic stay. "Nineteen was a tough year—for anybody, whether you're an actress or cramming for exams or your parents are driving you crazy or you're breaking up with your first love. Whatever you're going through, it's a tough year."[3]

The normal emotional wear and tear of the age was exacerbated by the grim nature of *House of the Spirits*. "I was playing a political prisoner and I was doing torture scenes in Portugal. I came back and I was so tired— I've always been a terrible insomniac—and I was so exhausted. I was convinced I was having a nervous breakdown. So I checked myself in for sleep deprivation. Ryder says she had one hour of group therapy a day. "I really got nothing from it," she said of the experience. "Those places don't really help . . . which is incredibly upsetting when you think that you can."[4]

Originally, she had thought that if she paid them enough, surely they could give her some kind of cure for feeling "broken." "But it didn't work like that," she said. "I left there feeling just the same, pretty much, and just as tired." The biggest irony to Ryder was that the emotionally draining torture scenes that had prompted her to check into the clinic were cut from the film before *House of the Spirits* was released.[5]

Although the hospital didn't help her directly, she did have an important epiphany—that she was the only one who could solve her problems. "Just because life is weird and messy doesn't mean I have to be miserable," she remarks. "Knowing this has gotten me through a lot of demons and darkness that tried to enter my life."[6]

A couple of years later, Ryder was given the galley proofs for Kaysen's book; they struck her like a branding iron. "Susan's book spoke to me on a very personal level. It just really captured a mood—that time in your life that is so confusing and so lonely and so oddly funny and weird. It was brutally honest without being self-indulgent. She articulated feelings I hadn't been able to."[7]

Ryder had begun acting when she was 12. Her small movie roles had evolved into more prominent ones in films such as *Beetlejuice*, *Heathers*, and *Edward Scissorhands*, the film where she met Johnny Depp. Unlike many other child actors, Ryder seemed to make the transition to adult roles with little difficulty, moving into films such as *The Age of Innocence*, *Reality Bites*, and *Alien Resurrection*. She considered *Girl, Interrupted* as her way "of exiting adolescence. It's a farewell piece to that time in my life, to all of those roles that I had. I just didn't realize it was going to take seven years to make."[8]

By the time the film was produced, Ryder was in her late 20s with a more mature perspective on her character. Reflecting her own epiphany, Ryder felt that the events portrayed in the film help her character realize that a certain amount of craziness is normal and that it's alright to be confused.[9]

One of Mangold's biggest challenges was writing an adaptation that didn't lose the sense of place the book had captured. Mangold was committed to being loyal to the feelings and themes of the book.[10] To help preserve the book's essence, he took the creative liberty of expanding the other characters mentioned in the book, especially Lisa, a charming sociopath who revels in troublemaking and button-pushing. To Mangold, Lisa symbolized a type of freedom that Susanna did not quite possess. "Some of what we think of as crazy is also just speaking the truth all the time," he explained. So to play Lisa, Mangold wanted an actress who, like Lisa, had no filter. "Those filters are what keep you from telling your boss he's an asshole."[11]

When he began the casting process, Mangold says he wondered if he would be able to find an actress capable of losing those social conventions believably, an actress brave enough. "All I knew was that the person had to be dangerous, highly verbal, and sexy—a kind of female De Niro," he said.[12]

It wasn't that he lacked for young women wanting the role. Nearly every actress in the right age range auditioned for the role, but none of them had the quality the director was looking for until Angelina Jolie walked into the room. She strode in without a word, plopped herself down on the office couch and looked at Mangold. In that instant, he realized he wasn't looking at Jolie, he was staring into the eyes of Lisa.

The director says auditioning Jolie for the role was one of the "greatest moments" of his life. "It was clear to me that day that I was watching someone who was not acting. There was someone speaking through her, it was a part of herself . . . I not only knew I had Lisa, but that I also had confidence in the movie I had written." Mangold took Angelina through every scene in the script where Lisa appears and at the end, he knew the search was over.[13]

Jolie had read *Girl, Interrupted* long before she auditioned for the movie. "When I read the script, it was that speech at the end that grabbed me, about *having buttons and pushing them and not feeling anything*," she says. "At that point in my life it was like a crying scream that I needed to have . . . I was very happy when I got it. I was screaming."[14]

Like Ryder, Jolie felt a primal understanding of what Kaysen was writing about. "I remember being very upset that I wasn't crazy, that I wasn't a vampire," Jolie says of her adolescence. "I wanted to be on stage and think I was someone else." After getting the role, Angelina says she went to the library and looked up sociopath, "and they said to look under serial killers. And you read about them and they're just not aware. They live on impulse so you can't analyze them. You have to throw the books away and say, *OK, what do I really feel right now?* and just do it. And sometimes you do things that you're pretty scared of."[15]

Her insatiable curiosity and courage is what most impressed Mangold about Jolie, who he calls *filterless*. A lot of actors can audition a good game, but Jolie, says the director, has substance to back her up. "Angie is rebellious, volatile and really smart," he says. "Playing this role put her in the mode of questioning authority. But if someone delivers the goods like she did, then I'm happy to struggle with the personality."[16]

Jolie doesn't deny she was confrontational during filming. "Acting is not pretending or lying. It's finding a side of yourself that's like the character and ignoring your other sides. And there's a side of me that wonders what's wrong with being completely honest. I get angry when I see people thinking they're better than others. So, yeah, she's a lot like me in a certain way."[17]

Playing a sociopath meant that Angelina had to curb her own natural compassion. For example, if Winona didn't feel well or had a headache,

Jolie would try to ignore that knowledge because her character felt nothing. The movie begins like the book. It's 1967, and 17-year-old Susanna is sent to a private mental hospital by a psychiatrist she barely knows, although it's clear from the outset she is more sane than many of her fellow teenage patients, who include a pathological liar (Clea Duvall), a burn victim who has decided to remain a child (Elisabeth Moss), and a neurotic laxative addict with a daddy complex (Brittany Murphy). It is Lisa, though, who will be the key to Susanna's journey back to the real world.

Filming the movie was an incredibly intense, difficult and perhaps cathartic experience for Jolie. "The movie takes place in the Sixties, and just learning what they did to people back then is horrifying. There's one girl in there because she's gay. I wish they'd focused more on that character. It's so sad to think that someone was given shock treatments just because they're unsure of their sexuality."[18]

It also proved difficult for Jolie to feel as comfortable with her cast mates as she had been on other films—she admitted that she generally doesn't get along with women. She recalled in a *Harper's Bazaar* interview an incident where one of the other actresses felt snubbed by Jolie. She admits that her lack of sensitivity can hurt women's feelings too much, but the drama of it annoyed Jolie, who says this kind of thing doesn't happen with male co-stars.[19] "If I come on set and my character has a particularly heavy scene that day, no guy has ever come up to me, you know, like, *You were really rude to me yesterday*. But that happens sometimes with girls."[20]

However, Jolie denied she had any personality conflicts with Ryder, as a few news reports suggested.[21] In fact, both Jolie and Ryder stayed so in character that they had little interaction off the set. "It was rare to see either of them out of character for the entire 12-week shoot," says Brittany Murphy, who played Daisy. In the movie, Lisa dislikes Daisy so between takes Murphy says Jolie "shunned me. One day, she began talking to me and then stopped cold. She stared hard at me and Angelina was replaced by Lisa and she walked away. She was always teasing me about the wig I had to wear for Daisy. At the end of the shoot she gave me a backpack with a dog that had exactly the same hairstyle. I think it was her way of telling me there were no hard feelings. It was just part of her acting process."[22] Ryder was equally introverted, never acknowledging the other actors on a day-to-day basis.

Jolie suspects she might not have been the most enjoyable company during filming. "I know our characters were very different, and I think in many ways it was scarier for her to play that role," Angelina says of Ryder. "I took on a personality so full of force, and she took on a personality that was scared, so the two of us together . . . I'm sure I was not lovely in the morning to her, you know. But I was very proud of her. I was very proud of how much this affected her, how hard she worked. I'm a little crazy probably in comparison. I'm a little out of my mind."[23]

Playing someone dangling over the edge does take a toll. Nevertheless, Jolie describes the experience as being "so unsettling it was settling." Jolie says she understood Lisa completely and didn't need to make her crazy. Instead, she just lived on impulse, not feeling much. "I have this quote from Tennessee Williams tattooed on my upper arm. It says, *A prayer for the wild at heart kept in cages*. That's Lisa. That's me," she said.[24] Angelina credits her director for keeping her from spiraling too much out of control.

The pre-release buzz surrounding Jolie's performance in *Girl, Interrupted* helped give the movie an added bit of notoriety, but there was some concern about how people would respond to such an intense film. "Everything out there now is a commercial, teen movie," says producer Cathy Konrad, who is married to Mangold. "The dramas are few and far between."[25] Neverthesless, Columbia was so convinced that Jolie's performance was award-worthy, the film was given a one-week December release in order to qualify for 1999 Academy Award consideration. Critics gave the filmmakers credit for tackling the subject matter but were almost uniformly blown away by Jolie, who received the best reviews of her already well-reviewed career.

"*Girl, Interrupted* is shrewd, tough, and lively," wrote *Entertainment Weekly* reviewer Owen Gleiberman. "Most of the patients are harmless, but Lisa (Angelina Jolie), a heartless, charismatic sociopath, delights in her destructive power. Jolie brings the kind of combustible sexuality to the screen that our movies, in the age of Meg Ryan, have been missing for too long."[26]

Geoff Pevere of the *Toronto Star* wrote, "The film suffers because its main character doesn't suffer enough. Which is why Jolie, bringing to her performance . . . something of the glassy-eyed suicide-chic she demonstrated in the TV-biopic *Gia*, wipes the hospital floors with Ryder whenever Lisa's around."[27]

For *Newsday*'s Gene Seymour, "Jolie livens things up, even—or especially—when Lisa's being very bad. Alone among the cast, she seems to have emerged from a time warp straight from the 1960s, oozing the sexy, scary recklessness of that era. Ryder is well cast and keeps things anchored. Even at her best, she never makes you forget her star persona the way Jolie does."[28]

Perhaps most critics felt the same as Chris Vognar of *The Dallas Morning News* when he called Jolie "a dangerous live wire." He wrote, "The part should finally cement Ms. Jolie's status as one of the most convincing young actresses around, one of the few who can disappear without a trace into a tough role."[29]

Despite the accolades heaped on Angelina, she seemed determined not to be taken in. It was almost as if she feared that without her angst and turmoil, she would lose that fuel that stoked her creative muse.

NOTES

1. Tricia Lanie, "Girl Talk: Hollywood's Actresses Are Abuzz about the Film Version of *Girl, Interrupted*," *Entertainment Weekly*, October 23, 1998.

2. Bob Ivry, "Relatively Secret," *Record*, April 25, 1999, http://www.highbeam.com/doc/1P1-24208016.html.

3. Bruce Kirkland, "Winona Ryder's Talking Crazy," http://jam.canoe.ca/Movies/Artists/R/Ryder_Winona/1999/12/20/761356.html.

4. *Girl, Interrupted* Press Junket. December 1999, Los Angeles. Author attended.

5. Ibid.

6. Ibid.

7. Jessica Holt, "'Girl' Offers Comfort for Misunderstood," *Daily Bruin*, January 10, 2000, http://ryder.fan-sites.org/2000january10_dailybruinonline.htm.

8. Chris Norris, "Say Goodbye to the Brooding Gen-Xer: Winona Ryder Has Grown into a Woman of Impeccable Taste," *In Style*, January 2, 2000.

9. Amy Longsdorf, "Woman on the Verge," *Playboy*, http://www.playboy.co.uk/page/WomenOnTheVerge/0,,11569~766428,00.html.

10. Holt, "'Girl' Offers Comfort."

11. Ibid.

12. "Girl Uncorrupted," EntertainmentWeekly.com, http://members.fortunecity.com/foxdm/id68.htm.

13. Anne Bergman, "A Proverbial Adventurer," *Los Angeles Times*, November 17, 1999.

14. Steve Goldman, "Angelina Jolie," *Total Film*, March 2000.

15. Holt, "'Girl' Offers Comfort."

16. Jeffrey Ressner, "Rebel without a Pause," *Time*, January 24, 2000, http://www.time.com/time/magazine/article/0,9171,37644,00.html.

17. Ibid.

18. Longsdorf, "Woman on the Verge."

19. Deanna Kizis, "Truth and Consequences," *Harper's Bazaar*, November 1999, http://fansites.hollywood.com/~ajolie/int15.html.

20. Ibid.

21. Trish Deitch Rohrer, "Dangerous Beauties: Winona Ryder and Angelina Jolie Walk on the Wild Side," *Premiere*, October 1999, http://www.hollywood.com/news/Winona_Interrupted/311849.

22. Louis B. Hobson, "Going by Murphy's Law," Jam.com, http://jam.canoe.ca/Movies/Artists/M/Murphy_Brittany/2000/01/09/760428.html.

23. *Girl, Interrupted* press kit. Columbia Pictures, December 1999.

24. Ibid.

25. Ibid.

26. Owen Gleiberman, "Review of *Girl, Interrupted*," *Entertainment Weekly*, January 7, 2000.

27. Geoff Peveref, "*Girl* an Unsatisfying Minor Interruption," *Toronto Star*, December 21, 1999.

28. Gene Seymour, "Disorder in the Ward: A Memoir of a Teen Mental Institution," *Newsday*, December 21, 1999.

29. Chris Vognar, "On the Edge: Story of a Young Woman's Breakdown Is Both Dark and Illuminating," *Dallas Morning News*, January 14, 2000.

Chapter 10

GOLDEN MOMENTS

For the third time in her young career, Jolie won a Golden Globe, this time for Best Performance by an Actress in a Supporting Role. To the curiosity of the onlookers in the audience, she dragged her brother James to the stage with her to accept. When the nominations for the Academy Awards were announced the following month, Jolie was expected to be a shoe-in for a Best Supporting Actress nomination. On one of her biggest days as a professional actor, Jolie was thousands of miles away in Mexico filming *Dancing in the Dark*. When she was finally reached for comment, Angelina said, "All the women in my category are so cool. . . . I just feel so lucky today."[1]

As the date of the Oscars approached, Jolie couldn't help but get caught up in the anxiety of the pending big night. "I get nervous and don't eat as much," she admitted in an Interview with Australia's *Sunday Mail*.

When Sunday, March 26 finally arrived, Jolie looked relieved it would soon be over, in one fashion or another. She arrived at the ceremony with her brother James, clutching him amidst the photographer's blinding flashbulbs and the din of people calling her name.

Jolie was so distracted by the activity surrounding her, she ended up getting locked out of the auditorium for 20 minutes until the first commercial break. Worried she was going to miss the Best Supporting Actress announcement, which is traditionally the ceremony's first award, Jolie pleaded with security to be admitted. Her biggest concern was how disappointed her mother would be. Finally, actor James Coburn, who was presenting her category, got them in.

Jolie was glad she wouldn't have to wait hours for her category. As was expected by nearly everybody, she won. Angelina looked dumbstruck. She reached over and gave her brother, who had tears streaming down his face, a rather long, on-the-lips kiss before making her way to the podium. "I'm surprised nobody's ever fainted up here," she said with a quiver to her voice. "I'm . . . I'm in shock. And I'm so in love with my brother right now. He just held me and said he loved me. And I know he's so happy for me. And thank you for that. And thank you to Columbia. Winona, you're amazing, and thank you for supporting all of us through this. And all the girls in this film are amazing . . . my mom who is the most brave, beautiful woman I've ever known. And my dad. You're a great actor, but you're a better father. And Jamie, you're just—I have nothing without you. You are the strongest, most amazing man I've ever known. And I love you. And thank you so much."[2]

Backstage, Jolie gripped her award, still seeming dazzled. When asked if she ever worried about going too far with a role, she laughed. "Oh, I think I'm never concerned about going too far because I've never seen anybody do that . . . It was always amazing to me when I see people just be free and not care if they're judged, so I kind of counted on people to have a fire in them as however too much it was or silly it was."[3]

Although most people knew the movie was based on an autobiography, few realized Jolie was in contact with the woman on whom her character was based. When asked about the woman on Oscar night, Jolie said, "She hasn't decided to be in very much contact with me. I'm thinking she probably won't until all of this blows over with all of you. She's living her life. At the end of the book, she had a child, a boy, so that child is probably around my age now. And I think she's in New York, but I would guess she's gone through a lot, and she's kind of maybe just now settling."[4]

Hinting at her previous escapades at the Golden Globes years earlier, somebody asked if she was upset there was no pool at the Shrine Auditorium, where the ceremony was held. Jolie smiled devilishly and acknowledged that without a pool, she would certainly try to find another way to live out her excitement.[5]

On a more serious note, she also reflected on the thoughts that had rushed through her head when she heard her name announced. "I really didn't expect it," she admitted. "I just hid in my brother's arms, and I think in both of our minds we both were just like, *Oh, my.* We grew up in this business, and dad has an Oscar, and it's like the big thing you try to attain as an actor, to do a performance that's really acknowledged and means something."[6] Surprisingly, Jolie says she had never held an Oscar before she won hers. "It's quite amazing. My dad's mother had his in a goldfish bowl, or something, on the mantelpiece in New York. It was way up in something. And I've never held it. Growing up with it, you figure it's the strange thing in grandma's house."[7]

Considering the role in retrospect, Jolie reflected that she knew she was right for the part of Lisa because she was so scared of playing the role. She had had the same reluctance about *Gia*, fearing that the role exposed her too much. For the part of Lisa, however, Jolie was scared for a different reason. When she read the script, Lisa's parts made her cry. "Different things I read, it hurt me," Jolie reflected. "It was important to me, and I didn't even want to go over the lines because I was deeply affected by her." However, she decided that it was important that somebody speak for Lisa. "I wanted her to have a voice," she explained.[8]

As questions wore on, Jolie's thoughts turned more and more to her family. She told reporters that earlier that day, her parents had brought her gifts before the ceremony. In Jolie's eyes, the gifts said, "*We love you and we're proud of you* from the whole family."

The Academy Awards were also an important milestone for her parents as well. Angelina recounted that when she had told her mother that she needed a new car, her mom had become nostalgic. "*But you went on all of your auditions in this car, you lost a hundred jobs in this car*," Angelina recounts her mother saying. "And she got emotional and said, *Can you believe you're going to the Oscars?* You know, that's my mom. My dad came in and said he was proud of me and that I was a good actress. To hear that from your father, for him to think I'm a good actress is kind of a big deal to me, so that was all I needed, and he loved me, and that's all that mattered."[9]

Voight also brought Marcheline a gift, thanking her for helping guide their daughter's career.[10] Jolie would later recall that when she called her mom from backstage, "she was having a f***ing heart attack. My father had called her—he'd been at Spago waiting for me—and apparently the two of them were on the phone crying, which is wonderful. When they saw me say to my brother, *I love you*, they saw how much their two children love each other and how we're going to be okay always because we have each other. So they were, like, out of their minds."[11]

When asked about her closeness to her brother, Jolie looked thoughtful. "Oh, God, well, I don't know if it's divorced families or what it is, but he and I were each others' everything, always, and we've been best friends. Maybe it's just my brother but he's been always my strongest support, and he's the funniest person I know. He's the sweetest human being I know. He's a good person, and he's just given me so much love and taken care of me, and you know, it makes life great. He's my friend."[12]

Looking at the entirety of Angelina's life, hearing her speak about the love she feels for her brother seems in keeping with the intensity with which she experiences life. James was the older brother who encouraged Angelina to act, who filmed her in home movies, and who kept her company growing up. She was acutely aware that her career had rocketed past his but it wasn't fun if she couldn't bring him along for the ride and in turn, encourage and support him as he looked to make his own mark. This is one of the reasons he has appeared in many of her films in small roles. However, when briefly viewed within the context of Oscar night, her professions of love and affection raised eyebrows, and in the weeks and months that followed, Angelina and James were suddenly the focus of media speculations concerning incest.

"It's a really weird thing," Haven expressed to Elizabeth Snead of *USA Today*. "I laughed at first, then I got angry about it. Now that I have had time to think, I think it's just that people are not used to this, so they automatically think negatively. But everyone who has jumped to this very sick thought is going to have egg on their face. They are writing all these stories that will be there forever, and they will realize in time that it is just a very close relationship and it has nothing to do with what they are implying."[13]

"I did not give Angie a French kiss, it was something simple and lovely," he says. "I congratulated her on the Oscar win and gave her a quick kiss on the lips. It was snapped and became a big thing round the world." Making light of the situation, Haven teased that he was thinking of getting his first tattoo that would read *Angelina*.[14]

Jolie was more exasperated. "God, that rumor was so predictable. I knew that one was coming. I could have written that story myself." Then she added pointedly, "The thing is, if I *were* sleeping with my brother, I would tell people I was. People know that about me."[15]

What the rest of the world *didn't* know was that Angelina was already deeply embroiled in a passionate, secret affair. However, it would be several months before she would go public with the relationship.

HEALING

Instead of taking time off after her Oscar win, she decided to accept a role in the Nicholas Cage film, *Gone in 60 Seconds* about a master car thief forced to pull off one more heist to save his brother. Angelina said she accepted the role because it was more play than work. After the emotionally draining work of *Girl, Interrupted*, Angelina wanted some time to just hang out and be silly. "I needed to be around Nic and those guys, who are really nice people, and just have a really silly time with them," she explained.[16]

While the movie appealed to her because it was fun, many people wondered why she would accept a role in a seemingly frivolous action flick. "It's like they expect more from you and that's terrible," she lamented. "I just wanted to play. And I wanted to be around a lot of men. I'd been around women in a mental institution for way too long." Plus, as she admits, "If I'm not working, I'm not focused. It's where I feel useful."[17]

Gone in 60 Seconds was a $100 million remake of H. B. Halicki's 1974 cult classic and was little more than summer popcorn fare—lots of cars and crashes. Jolie doesn't appear on screen until midway through the two-hour film. In addition to seeing the film as a kind of working vacation, Jolie says it was a great opportunity to learn about cars. "I know how to steal a car now, although maybe I shouldn't get that out there. We actually had a real thief on the set, escorted by his prison guard. I asked the thief a million questions and this guy could rip apart an entire car and tell you every single part of it," Jolie marveled.[18]

For the most part, *Gone in 60 Seconds* didn't make a splash. Critics barely wasted ink on reviewing it and most reviews took the tone of salon. com critic Dave Thompson, who quipped, "*Gone in 60 Seconds* isn't just rubbish, it's Nicolas Cage and PG-13 rubbish." Despite blowing off the film, he did have a few kind words for Jolie. "Angelina Jolie is another matter. She's the kind of treasure that no one has the least idea how to handle . . . She has in her own way what very few American women have had—Louise Brooks, Jean Harlow, Tuesday Weld, Marilyn Monroe—and what they were seldom allowed to deliver."[19]

She also had that certain something that makes the wives of actors very nervous. While filming *Dancing in the Dark*, there were published reports that Antonio Banderas's wife, Melanie Griffith, was less than pleased with the movie's sex scenes between her husband and Jolie. However, Angelina dismissed the rumors out of hand. "Melanie has absolutely no reason to worry about me. I'm not the type to prey on a married man," she asserted. She also pointed out, "I've had more on-screen relationships with men than I've had off-screen in my entire life."[20]

Angelina neglected to mention that the reason she had no interest in Banderas was that she had already found someone.

In January 2000, Jolie had spoken like a person resigned to being alone. Since her divorce from Miller, she dated here and there, but emotionally, she felt alone. In other interviews, Jolie would take responsibility for her singleness, acknowledging that because she worked so much, it was hard to maintain any kind of serious relationship. In her opinion, it simply wasn't fair to the other person since she was unable to be there physically, and was often emotionally distant as a result of her work.[21] Nevertheless, she claimed to be very happy on her own. "I have a lot of really great male friends so I don't feel I need intimacy," she observed.[22] On the other hand, she didn't stop fantasizing. "When I was young, my dad and I watched Marlon Brando in A *Streetcar Named Desire*," she remembered. "I told my dad that was the kind of animal passion I wanted from a man."[23]

However, throughout her life, relationships had been difficult. Angelina had her first sexual relationship when she was 14.[24] Her boyfriend lived with her in her mother's house and they had a serious relationship for two years.[25] During this time, Jolie experimented with cutting herself; in retrospect, she says the cutting was a response to feeling emotionally numb. Once, she and her boyfriend experimented with knife-play. "We attacked each other," she explained. "It felt so primitive and it felt so honest—and then I had to deal with, you know, not telling my mother, hiding things, wearing gauze bandages to high school."[26]

Looking back, Jolie believes her phase of self-mutilation was the result of teenage angst and ennui. "But by the time I was 16," she says with a laugh, "I had gotten it all out of my system."[27]

While she may have gotten over the urge to hurt herself with knives, her past relationships still pained her. Jolie's divorce from Miller wasn't finalized until the filming of Gone in 60 Seconds. Even though it was old territory, the finality of it still pained Angelina. The pain of the divorce, combined with the emotional weight from Girl, Interrupted, as well as other personal matters that included a close friend's illness, conspired to make her almost physically ill. Her face broke out, she lost weight, and her emotions were on edge. One day, the Gone in 60 Seconds director suggested she go home and take care of herself and her previous openness about drug experimentation prompted whispered speculation.

The emotionally trying time also made Angelina realize how alone she was. "I just went through an emotional time," she says, "But when you do that in this business, you realize the ugliness of what the worst in their eyes would be; that people are thinking that you're sick. If in the future I ever was, this is how little people would help me," she realized. Although Jolie claimed that everyone in Gone in 60 Seconds was great to her, the experience still "made me yearn for a normal life."[28]

Although she was still only in her mid-twenties, Jolie began to spend more interview time musing about settling down and having children. On more than one occasion, she expressed an interest in adopting a child, adding that she had no desire to get pregnant and give birth. But before committing to a child, she hoped to find a life partner.

When it came to life partners, Jolie claimed that a little craziness was really sexy, and that a few scars and mistakes were important. "I don't like perfect, plastic looks," she said.[29] And as far as passion goes, Jolie wanted it to be "a combination of thinking, *I love you but I just want to rip that apart and eat you.*" While she said she hadn't found that yet, she did say she had had signs. She regarded her relationship with Miller as sort of an "honest experiment," but considered that it might be the not everyone finds that crazy, passionate love she craved.[30]

Nevertheless, between the time *Gone in 60 Seconds* was filmed and the time it was released in June 2000, Angelina Jolie fell in love. And this was not the sweetness and light, hearts and flowers kind of valentine love. It was the go-out-of-your-mind, be-afraid-of-losing-control kind of crazy love she had always wanted.

NOTES

1. Arlene Vigoa, "And the First Time Nominees Are . . . ," *USA Today*, March 20, 2000, http://www.usatoday.com/life/special/oscar2000/osc05.htm.

2. Author in attendance. Shrine Auditorium, Los Angeles, March 26, 2000.

3. Angelina Jolie, informal press conference, The Shrine Auditorium, Los Angeles, California, March 26, 2000.

4. Ibid.

5. Ibid.

6. Ibid.

7. Ibid.

8. Ibid.

9. "Angelina in Love," *Talk*, June/July 2000, http://fansites.hollywood.com/~ajolie/int6.html.

10. Angelina Jolie, informal press conference.

11. "Angelina in Love."

12. Angelina Jolie, informal press conference.

13. Sharon Feinstein, "My Sister Angelina's Secret Sadness," *Mail on Sunday*, March 25, 2007, http://www.highbeam.com/doc/1P2-13554319.html.

14. Oliver O'Neil, "The Wild and Wacky World of Angelina Jolie, Tomb Raider," *Planet Syndication*, http://www.unreel.co.uk/features/featureangelinajoliepage3.cfm.

15. Ray Pride, "That Girl: An Interview with Actress Angelina Jolie," DrDrew.com, 2000, http://www.drdrew.com/DrewLive/article.asp?id=406.

16. Beatboxbetty, "Angelina Jolie—Gone in 60 Seconds," Beatboxbetty.com, http://www.beatboxbetty.com/celebetty/angelinajolie/angelinajolie2/angelinajolie2.htm.

17. Pride, "That Girl."

18. Cindy Pearlman, "A Jolie Good Time," *Daily Telegraph*, June 10, 2000.

19. David Thompson, "Drive Us Wild, Angelina," *Salon*, June 14, 2000.

20. Drew Mackenzie and Ivor Davis, "I'm Both Sinister and Soft," *Woman's Day* (Australia), April 17, 2000, http://zone.ee/daart/ar42.html.

21. Louis B. Hobson, "Jolie's Rocky Relationships," *Calgary Sun*, January 9, 2000, http://www.jonnyleemiller.co.uk/angelinajolie.html.

22. Louis B. Hobson, "Angie, Committed." *Edmonton Sun*, January 9, 2000.

23. Hobson, "Jolie's Rocky Relationships."

24. Andrei Harmsworth, "I Was Sexual at Nursery Age." April 18, 2007, http://www.metro.co.uk/fame/article.html?in_article_id=45770&in_page_id=7.

25. Karen S. Schneider, "Girl, Undaunted," *People*, June 25, 2001, http://www.people.com/people/archive/article/0,,20134761,00.html.

26. Stephen M. Silverman, "Angelina Jolie Airs Colorful Past on TV," *People*, July 09, 2003, http://www.people.com/people/article/0,,626414,00.html.

27. Schneider, "Girl, Undaunted."

28. Deanna Kizis, "What the Hell Is Wrong with Angelina Jolie?," *Jane*, February 2000, http://angelanna3.tripod.com/interviews2000/id3.html.

29. Louis B. Hobson, "Pushing Her Luck," *Calgary Sun*, April 18, 1999, http://jam.canoe.ca/Movies/Artists/J/Jolie_Angelina/1999/04/18/759417.html.

30. Kizis, "What the Hell Is Wrong with Angelina Jolie?"

Chapter 11

COMBUSTIBLE

Since 1999, Jolie had been quietly seeing actor Billy Bob Thornton. When the news broke officially, their romance not only took the public and media by surprise, but reportedly Thornton's longtime-girlfriend, Laura Dern, as well. As with any story like this, it's difficult to separate fact from fiction, because once it becomes public, everyone tends to put their own spin on it. What is known for sure is that Billy Bob and Angelina met during the spring of 1998 while filming *Pushing Tin*. Jolie admitted later that she was interested in Thornton from the first time they met. "When I first met him I was in shock," she remembered. Although nothing happened at the time, Angelina recalls being struck with Thornton. "I just went on with my life, but I never really forgot . . . I never enjoyed anybody just sitting and talking."[1]

Jolie alluded that their romance didn't begin in earnest until later because she didn't know if it would be possible. "I liked him too much to think he should ever be near somebody like me," she remarked. "I just didn't think much of myself. I wanted to be better as a person."[2]

Nevertheless, by March 2000, the relationship had turned romantic. Not only was Angelina spotted with a new tattoo that read *Billy Bob*, she was flying into Los Angeles every chance she could from the Mexican location of *Dancing in the Dark*. She also spent some time with Thornton after the Oscar ceremony before catching a 4:00 A.M. plane back to Mexico. As far as how she managed to keep people from knowing, she says, "I don't think anybody was looking for it!"[3]

Certainly not Laura Dern, who had been involved with Thornton ever since the actor had split from his fourth wife, Pietra Dawn, shortly after the 1997 Academy Awards ceremony where he received an Oscar for his *Sling Blade* screenplay. The ensuing divorce proceedings between Thornton and Dawn were bitter, with her accusing Billy Bob of physical abuse and describing him as a manic-depressive who turned violent when he stopped taking his lithium. The finger-pointing became so heated, with each accusing the other of making death threats, that the presiding judge issued a restraining order against both of them.[4]

Putting the past aside, Billy Bob and Angelina were married in a 20-minute Las Vegas ceremony at the Little Church of the West on May 5, 2000. Chapel owner Greg Smith told the Associated Press that the bride and groom both wore blue jeans. It was Thornton's fifth marriage. According to reports, Thornton and Jolie were accompanied by Billy Bob's best friend, Harve Cook, who served as the Best Man. Nobody from Jolie's family was present. Their wedding package cost $200 and included the ceremony, performed by the Reverend James Hamilton, photos, flowers—a bouquet of roses and carnations—and music ("Unchained Melody," by the Righteous Brothers).

The newlyweds were enraptured with one another. "Angelina is everything to me as a human being, as an artist and as a partner," Thornton gushed. "I was looking at her sleep and I had to restrain myself from literally squeezing her to death. Sex for us is almost too much."[5]

At the June 5, 2000, premiere of *Gone in 60 Seconds*, Jolie and Thornton arrived arm-in-arm, unable to keep their hands off one another. Like Thornton, Jolie was unable to stop talking about the man she referred to as the love of her life. "I wasn't a great wife before. But I finally came to a place where I hope I can make somebody happy." The power of love also brought out some other characteristics that were new for Angelina. "I've never known what it was to be jealous, obsessive; wanting to talk constantly . . . I used to feel that my work was why I was alive. Now I feel there is something more special. I used to not be afraid to die. Now I'm so happy living. I don't want to miss a moment."[6]

Jolie also talked about feeling more grounded as a person since her involvement with Thornton. In press interviews she described herself as more content and alive, claiming that Thornton's strength let her feel proud of herself, safe, and centered. But Angelina wasn't oblivious to the skepticism of outsiders. "You know you always expect a certain amount of criticism and we've had that too, but we are very much in love and we are going to share our lives with people. We don't mind. And we hope people are rooting for us rather than being against us," she said.[7]

Even if the critics weren't rooting for her, Angelina was convinced Thornton was her life mate. Angelina also defended Thornton's marital track record by saying, "If I didn't meet him until I was older, during those years I probably would have been married four times, too. This is different. I know we've found each other now." And if she couldn't convince people of that—too bad. "It's not my responsibility to have a personal life that everybody's comfortable with."[8]

For as much as her marriage changed her personal life, it also put her professional life in new perspective. When she was single, work not only helped her mature and grow as a person, it filled a void caused by loneliness. Now with Thornton in her life, Jolie was looking to work less so she could stay home more. But first, Angelina had one last film commitment to fulfill—a potential cinematic blockbuster called *Tomb Raider*, which was filming in London.

If ever there was a film role that could succeed in both stretching Jolie's screen persona in new directions and catapulting her into the acting stratosphere reserved for the likes of Tom Cruise and Harrison Ford, it was portraying *Tomb Raider* heroine Lara Croft. In this age of digital convergence, Croft is truly a star of the future, a video game character that is revered as much as if she were flesh and blood. As the leading character in the *Tomb Raider* video game series, she was openly created as a female Indiana Jones. The back-story created for the games gave filmmakers a wealth of material to use for their movie script.

With a mane of dark hair that complements her 34D-24-35 figure on an impossibly lean and toned 5'9" frame, Croft's physical appeal is only matched by a toughness honed during her adventures as an archeologist. Croft is a hero who can alternately seduce an enemy with a flick of her head or shoot them.

Although Croft embodies many American traits—she would not be someone to trifle with during rush-hour traffic, for example—Lara is actually a British blueblood, known in aristocratic circles as the Duchess of Saint Bridget, the daughter of Lord Henshingly Croft. Born on Valentine's Day 1967 in Wimbledon, England, Lara was schooled at Gordonstoun Boarding School from the age of 16 to 18, and then spent three years at a Swiss finishing school.

While in Switzerland, Croft developed a love of skiing and spent time in the Himalayas searching out the most challenging runs she could find. On the way back from her holiday, however, the plane crashed deep within the mountains. Lara was the sole survivor. She spent the next two weeks learning to survive and when she finally found her way to a mountain village, Croft was a profoundly different person. Suddenly, her aristocratic upbringing seemed stifling and she craved to relive the exhilarating sensation of traveling alone and surviving by her own wits and cunning.

This personal catharsis was met less than enthusiastically by her parents, who had hoped Lara would marry the Earl of Farringdon. Hoping to bring her back to her aristocratic senses, Lara's parents cut off her allowance. However, there was no going back for their daughter—her life as an adventurer and "tomb raider" beckoned. While in England, Lara lives in a mansion in Surrey, which she inherited many years ago. Because she travels so much, the manse is used primarily to house all the artifacts she has acquired on her adventures. She has also had a custom-built assault course constructed in the grounds for training purposes.

Lara doesn't consider tomb raiding as a job, per se; to her it's a way of life. Even so, she has been known to seek out archeological artifacts on commission. Primarily, though, she earns money writing travel books, including *A Tyrannosaurus is Jawing at My Head* and *Slaying Bigfoot*. Lara gets the stories for her books from her real-life exploits, which have gained her worldwide notoriety. Not only has she uncovered many notorious archeological sites such as the Atlantean pyramid and the last resting place of the dagger of Xian, Lara has proven her mettle by driving the dangerous Alaskan Highway from Tierra del Fuego in South America in record time (although this was later denounced by the Guinness Book of Records due to her "reckless driving") and seeking out and killing Bigfoot. The biggest problem she has with writing is finding the time to write down all her adventures. Her primary interest remains discovering the undefined world of tombs and the past.

Lara Croft became an instant worldwide phenomenon when she made her debut in the 1996 action game *Tomb Raider*. Assertive, resourceful, and independent, Lara is arguably the first true virtual celebrity. She has appeared on over 200 magazine covers around the world; she was profiled in a December 1999 feature in *Time* magazine and has also appeared in *Newsweek, Rolling Stone,* and *Entertainment Weekly's* "It" issue, which spotlighted the hundred most creative people in entertainment. *The London Times* recently devoted a special 16-page supplement to her and *Time Digital* included Lara on a list of the 50 cyber-elite in America, ranking her among Bill Gates, Andy Grove, Steve Jobs, and George Lucas.

And in a truly unprecedented event, *Details* magazine honored Lara, a non-human being, as one of the *Sexiest Women of the Year*.

Croft also nudged her way into the ether usually reserved for supermodels, appearing in television advertising campaigns in North America, Europe, and Asia. She is the subject of more than one thousand Internet fan sites—each created independently of Eidos, the company that manufactures the *Tomb Raider* games, and her merchandise includes action figures, comic books, and a clothing line. Lara's success has even inspired the world-famous Elite Modeling Agency to devote an entire division to developing virtual models, an innovation other companies are now pursuing also.

What's particularly remarkable about Croft is that just a few years prior to her debut, female action figures were considered a hard sell. The conventional wisdom was that game players only wanted good guys, bad guys—the operative word being *guys*—monsters and aliens. No women need apply. Lara Croft changed all that when Eidos Interactive introduced her as the Tomb Raider.

"Lara Croft has crossover appeal," said Eidos executive, Gary Keith. "The core audience, males in the 13–35 age bracket, love to see this beautiful, buxom woman running around. They prefer this eye candy to game heroes who are rendered into Arnold Schwarzeneggers." Eidos also discovered that Croft also appealed to women. "Women like Lara Croft because they perceive her as a role model: she's not only adventurous but very well-educated."[9]

Buxom and brainy—it proved to be a combination that helped make *Tomb Raider* one of the most successful video and PC games of all time. Paramount Studios, looking to have the next great action film franchise with *Tomb Raider*, gave the film a budget in excess of $100 million.

Until then, no video character had successfully made the transition to film. Many industry experts believed Croft would succeed where others failed because her character already had a complex personality and back story full of rich adventures.

As for Jolie, playing a video icon was a bit daunting. "Actually, I'm frightened about it," she admitted. "Do I look like an action hero?"[10]

Paul Baldwin, VP of marketing for Eidos recalls, "We signed the deal for the film back in 1997, and figured they'd cast some unknown in the part. Getting someone like Angelina Jolie was beyond our wildest dreams. Having an actor of her caliber is wonderful for the film, and she's got both the looks and the attitude for the part."[11]

Typically, it's the character Angelina responds to. "It's not going to be campy and stupid. She's tough and real and a warrior, so it's not going to be a cartoon or cute but it has a lot to do about our planet," she said, justifying her part.[12]

In order to train for the rigorous role, Jolie spent almost two months in England prior to the start of filming to get in shape. "I get up and do yoga at seven in the morning, which is insane! I'm on protein shakes and they've taken my cigarettes and alcohol and sugar away from me—and Billy—because I'm far away." In addition, Jolie said she was getting training in "bungee ballet" and was doing everything from weapons training with the Special Forces to kickboxing, soccer, and rowing. In addition, Jolie had to perfect a British accent and pass a crash course in etiquette. "I think that's really funny—me in manners class," she laughed.[13]

Whether due to her marriage to Thornton or just the maturity that comes with age, Jolie had grown as a person. Although she was fundamentally the same person she was when she briefly engaged in self-mutilation and wallowed in angst and bleakness, the way she dealt with her emotions and life had changed. Instead of hiding in her work, she saw that she could connect to the world around her through it.

"There was a time when I was wondering whether to live or die," she once revealed. "But go through something like that and you become fearless. Because you're at the edge of the road and you're going to commit to life. That's what makes you finally feel good."[14]

Unlike her screen persona, Jolie isn't nearly as close to the edge as her interviews and film roles might suggest. And regardless of how some may interpret what she says, Angelina only knows one way to communicate. "I'll share everything always because it's what I want. It helps me continue to do my work that way. And I've got nothing to hide."[15]

After filming *Tomb Raider*, Jolie's ability to communicate would put her in a position to help people on a global scale and transform her into a passionate philanthropist.

NOTES

1. "Angelina in Love," *Talk*, June/July 2000, http://fansites.hollywood.com/~ajolie/int6.html.

2. Ibid.

3. Beatboxbetty, "Angelina Jolie—Gone in 60 Seconds," Beatboxbetty.com, http://www.beatboxbetty.com/celebetty/angelinajolie/angelinajolie2/angelina jolie2.htm.

4. "The Crazy World of Billy Bob," *Daily Telegraph*, August 25, 2001, http://www. telegraph.co.uk/arts/main.jhtml?xml=/arts/2001/08/25/babob25.xml&page=2.

5. "Angelina Jolie Love Story" US Weekly http://www.angelfire.com/dc/lia/ajus.html.

6. Stephanie Mansfield, "Oscar-Winning Actress Angelina Jolie Says She's Putting Her Wild Past Behind Her," *USA Weekend*, June 11, 2000, http://www.usaweekend.com/00_issues/000611/000611jolie.html.

7. Beatboxbetty, "Angelina Jolie—Gone in 60 Seconds."

8. David Germain, "Angelina Jolie Brushes off Bad Press," *Dallas Morning News*, June 11, 2000.

9. Press Material.

10. Jack Stenze, "Get Reel: Can Angelina Jolie Make Lara Croft Soar on Screen?," *Entertainment Weekly*, April 14, 2000.

11. Press Material.

12. Ibid.

13. Beatboxbetty, "Angelina Jolie—Gone in 60 Seconds."

14. Alison Boleyn, "Celebrity Profile: Angelina Jolie," *Marie Claire*, February 2000.

15. Beatboxbetty, "Angelina Jolie—Gone in 60 Seconds."

Chapter 12

ACTRESS TURNED ACTIVIST

Her roles in *Gia* and *Girl, Interrupted* proved Jolie had serious acting chops; *Tomb Raider* made her an international box office star. After so many years of plumbing the emotional depths of her characters, Jolie's stint as an action hero was a breath of fresh air.

"This is the first time that I happened to do something that was mainstream," she noted in 2001. "Some people don't allow themselves to do something that is mainstream, even though they would love to try and have some fun with it, because they want to be credible and take themselves seriously. Certainly, in my life, I have drowned in being deep and complicated and dark. It's very hard sometimes to step up in life and be proud and be confident and be healthy and be strong and be adventurous and be light and to laugh. It's hard for me. It's hard to be free." Jolie says the whole point of *Tomb Raider* was to entertain the audience. In her opinion, entertainment can be as important as really complicated and deep films.[1]

Tomb Raider earned over $300 million worldwide, launching Jolie into rarified air usually reserved for male actors like Tom Cruise and Duane "The Rock" Johnson. Luckily, she made the transition without adopting a global-sized ego. Producer Lawrence Gordon noted, "Angelina is the perfect Lara Croft as far as we are concerned. In fact, I shudder to think who we would have gone with if Angelina had not done it . . . She could not have been easier to work with. She could not have been better in the role. And the amount of training and sheer guts that went into making this thing, for her, was enormous!"[2]

Tomb Raider director Simon West was equally smitten. Despite knowing her acting background, West was surprised at just how good she was. "She is one of those natural genius actresses," he marveled.[3]

While *Tomb Raider* was a milestone for Jolie professionally, it also marked her personal transformation from actress to humanitarian. She had never been comfortable being "a star" but Jolie learned she could leverage her celebrity into a force for good. The process had begun several years earlier. While in she was in Mexico shooting *Original Sin* she received a script for a movie titled *Beyond Borders*, a romantic drama about humanitarian workers in war-torn countries like Cambodia and Ethiopia.

Jolie says the script made her cry, and prompted her to take the role so that she could really understand the situation in those countries.[4] But then the production was put on hold. It had already undergone numerous changes and was in danger of being scrapped altogether. The original director had been Oliver Stone, with Kevin Costner and Catherine Zeta-Jones starring. Zeta-Jones dropped out after she became pregnant and was replaced by Meg Ryan, who subsequently dropped out. That was when Jolie was sent the script. Costner left the project and Ralph Fiennes signed on. But the producers wanted a more manly-man type actor so Fiennes was replaced by Clive Owen. Then Oliver Stone dropped out.

"I cried when I got the phone call that it wasn't going to happen," Jolie says, "and I had this moment of realizing, *Well, I'll just go! I'll take the journey. I'm a person. I'll go myself.*"[5]

Jolie researched aid relief and the United Nations, and then contacted the United Nations' High Commissioner for Refugees (UNHCR) and convinced them to let her travel to Sierra Leone, where a vicious civil war was being waged. She spent two weeks visiting refugee camps. The experience literally changed her life and she says she returned from that trip much better for the experience. "I would never complain again about the stupid things I used to, or be self-destructive, or not realize on a daily basis how lucky I am to have a roof over my head and enough food to eat," she elaborated.[6]

What had started as film research became a personal calling and the plight of refugees became the focus of Jolie's humanitarian efforts. In August 2001, she was appointed a United Nations goodwill ambassador at an event held in Geneva, Switzerland. Kris Janowski, spokesman for the U.N. High Commissioner for Refugees, said the actress was the kind of person who can get our message across to young people.[7]

An emotional Jolie recalled her visit to some of the Afghan refugees in Pakistan. Remembering homeless children scavenging for food in garbage dumpsters, she says that the experience is still hard to talk about, especially with the knowledge that there is no end in sight for many people in need. Jolie was impressed with their ability to maintain generous, kind dispositions despite their terrible situations.[8]

Soon, it became clear that Jolie wasn't just a U.N.-mouthpiece looking for good press. A month later, in September 2001, she donated $1 million to help Afghan refugees. In an official statement, High Commissioner Ruud Lubbers said, "This significant contribution from a concerned young American reinforces my belief that, despite the trauma of recent events in her country," referring to the September 11 terrorist attacks, "a strong sense of humanitarian responsibility toward innocent civilians suffering in far-off places continues to animate the spirit of caring individuals everywhere."[9]

That November, Jolie returned to Cambodia for a week, this time accompanied by Billy Bob Thornton. While there, she visited an orphanage and fell in love with a baby boy. "He was asleep," she recalls. "They put him in a bucket and poured water over him. He didn't wake up but they put him in my arms anyway. He opened his eyes and smiled at me. The connection was made that instant." Jolie immediately began the paperwork for adoption.[10]

Jolie and Thornton announced the finalized adoption on March 12, 2002, although only Jolie's name was on the adoption papers. At the time, Angelina was on location filming the long delayed *Beyond Borders*. Jolie named her new son Maddox. "He was only seven months old and there we were in the middle of Africa. I held him every moment the cameras weren't rolling."[11]

Four months later, Jolie and Thornton announced their divorce after only two years of marriage. While Angelina claims she was genuinely in love with Billy Bob when they got married, she admits that they grew apart until one day they were essentially strangers. She also stressed that adopting Maddox was not a factor in the break-up—their marriage was past saving by the time he came to live with them.

While her divorce from Miller had been emotionally painful because they were such good friends and still loved one another, Jolie says she felt little on dissolving her union with Thornton. "Billy Bob and I were no longer friends so it was just a matter of signing papers and moving on," she explained.[12]

While the break-up did not sour Jolie on relationships, it made her leery of marriage. "I have discovered that marriage is not my cup of tea," she said in 2003. "If I have a lover or friend in my life for a while, that will be a great bonus, but I don't have faith in the permanence of relationships and that is what marriage is all about. If I were to bring a man into my life now, he would have to be more than a husband. He would have to be a father to Maddox and that would have to be permanent. I wouldn't want Maddox to suffer watching his parents separating."[13]

Not long after her split from Thornton, Jolie became estranged from her father as well. On August 1, 2002, Voight appeared on *Access Hollywood* and accused Angelina of having serious mental problems. Calling himself "broken-hearted," he tearfully said, "I've been trying to reach my daughter and get her help, and I have failed and I'm sorry."[14] He also expressed grief that he had not been allowed to spend time with Maddox.

He also made similar comments on E! Entertainment Television, saying he had tried to get his daughter to see a psychiatrist. "I'm sorry I haven't come forward before and addressed her serious mental problems. But I have tried behind the scenes in every way . . . My daughter doesn't want to see me because I've made it very clear to her what the situation is and the help that she needs," he stated passionately.[15]

Jolie responded by issuing a statement to the press: "I don't want to make public the reasons for my bad relationship with my father. I will only say that, like every child, my brother Jamie and I would have loved to have had a warm and loving relationship with our dad. But after all these years, I have determined that it is not healthy for me to be around my father, especially now that I am responsible for my own child."[16]

NOTES

1. Bruce Kirkland, "She's Got Game," http://jam.canoe.ca/Movies/Artists/J/Jolie_Angelina/2001/06/10/759412.html.

2. Bruce Kirkland, "In Praise of Angelina Jolie," http://jam.canoe.ca/Movies/Artists/J/Jolie_Angelina/2001/06/15/759410.html.

3. Ibid.

4. Bruce Kirkland, "The New Angelina Jolie," http://jam.canoe.ca/Movies/Artists/J/Jolie_Angelina/2003/10/19/759420.html.

5. Ibid.

6. Ibid.

7. Stephen M. Silverman, "U.N. Honoring Goodwill Angelina Jolie," *People*, August 22, 2001.

8. Stephen M. Silverman, "Jolie Accepts U.N. Ambassador Post," *People*, August 28, 2001, http://www.people.com/people/article/0,,622486,00.html.

9. Stephen M. Silverman, "Angelina Jolie: $1 Mil to Refugees," *People*, September 28, 2001.

10. Louis B. Hobson, "The Jolly Life of Angelina," http://jam.canoe.ca/Movies/Artists/J/Jolie_Angelina/2003/07/20/759421.html.

11. Ibid.

12. Ibid.

13. Ibid.

14. Jon Voight, *Access Hollywood*, August 1, 2002.

15. Mark Reynolds, "Angelina's Troubles Are All My Fault Sobs Voight," *Daily Mail*, August 3, 2002, http://www.highbeam.com/doc/1P2-2247922.html.

16. Ibid.

Chapter 13

A GLOBAL FAMILY

While motherhood may have settled Jolie's soul, it did little to dampen her candor. Throughout her press interviews to promote *Alexander*, she was happy to tell anyone who asked that while her love life may be on hold, her sex life was very satisfying, thank you very much.

"I have two lovers right now and they're both men, for the moment anyway. As long as you have safe sex and you don't confuse your family, I think it's very healthy," she said, explaining that she had been friends with her lovers before becoming sexually involved with them. And she made clear from the start that the involvement was for companionship, not love. "You need to be very careful that no one gets hurt. I've been with one of them for two years now and we talk about life and politics, share books; now he's one of the greatest friends I have. Usually, there's a stereotype that women have to give their hearts in relationships, while men can just give their penises. But I don't believe that."[1]

As Maddox got older, Jolie's desire to give him siblings grew. She also revealed that Maddox was beginning to question what the word "daddy" meant. While she made it clear that she would love for Maddox to have a dad, she was committed to not settling for the wrong person. Now that Angelina had Maddox, she said, "What I'm looking for in a man has changed. Before, I was looking for a friend I could have fun with, be wild with, get lost with. Now, I'm looking for a man with the same morals as me, the same destiny as me, who can see raising children and approaching the world in the same way. I could never be with a man who was a bad father."[2]

Jolie also addressed rumors that she and her *Alexander* co-star Colin Farrell had an affair during filming. She admits they discussed the possibility of dating then decided they were too similar and made better friends than they would lovers.

Many journalists noted that Jolie, who had recently earned her pilot's license, seemed happier than she ever had in the past, an assessment she acknowledged. "I'm able to love acting now. In the past, I needed it because I was living vicariously through the characters I played. My characters always seemed to have lives more interesting than mine. Now, that's not the case and I can just show up on set and have a good time. I don't feel any pressure about how the film does or what the critics say," she clarified.[3]

Despite this new-found tranquility, Jolie was soon to be accused of being a home-wrecker.

On January 7, 2005, Brad Pitt and Jennifer Aniston announced in a statement issued to *People* magazine that they were separating after four and a half years of marriage.

"For those who follow these sorts of things, we would like to explain that our separation is not the result of any of the speculation reported by the tabloid media," Pitt and Aniston said. "This decision is the result of much thoughtful consideration. We happily remain committed and caring friends with great love and admiration for one another. We ask in advance for your kindness and sensitivity in the coming months."[4]

Almost immediately, media speculation pointed to Jolie as the reason for the split. In October 2004, paparazzi had photographed the pair in Italy where they were on location for their upcoming film, *Mr. and Mrs. Smith*. In the photo, Pitt and Jolie are simply walking together, but their body language suggested a comfortable intimacy. Tabloids began running stories about trouble brewing in the Pitt-Aniston marriage, claiming variously that Jennifer was insanely jealous of Jolie, that Pitt and Jolie had an on-location affair, that Brad was bitter Jennifer would not put her career on hold to have children, and that Aniston had caught Brad having phone sex with Jolie—all of which Pitt adamantly denied. However, it couldn't be denied that Pitt and Jolie began spending time together after his separation. In March, Aniston filed for divorce and by the time it was granted in August 2005, it was clear the relationship between Pitt and Jolie had surpassed that of friendship. Most telling were a series of photographs taken of Pitt playing with Maddox while the three were vacationing in Kenya.

It wouldn't be until after the birth of their daughter Shiloh that Jolie finally spoke publicly about the early days of their relationship, which began when they met during pre-production for *Mr. and Mrs. Smith* in early 2004. Jolie says that her only knowledge of Brad was from reading about him in the media. She also says they were the last two people looking to get involved. "I was quite content to be a single mom with Mad. And . . . it was clear he was with his best friend, someone he loves and respects. And so we were both living, I suppose, very full lives."[5]

Working together they became friends quickly. A few months into the production, Jolie says she realized that she was beginning to really look forward to going to work when she had to do something with Brad. She explained that they began to feel like a pair, even though neither of them fully realized the magnitude of what was happening until the end of the shoot. Knowing that it would be a huge thing for both of them, Jolie said they decided to wait and undertake any decision only after a lot of serious consideration.[6]

Like Pitt, Jolie says they did not have an affair. Knowing the heartbreak her mother suffered, she says she simply would not have an affair with a married man. Instead, she and Pitt developed their friendship. "We spent a lot of time contemplating and thinking and talking about what we both wanted in life and realized that we wanted very, very similar things. And then we just continued to take time."[7] Eventually, they decided they should be together—with a little help from Maddox.

"There was a coming together of him and Brad. It's a big thing to bring together a child and a father," she said. "It had never crossed my mind that Mad was going to need a father—certainly not that it would be this man I just met. Until, of course, I got to know Brad and realized that he is naturally just a wonderful father. And we left a lot of it up to Mad, and he took his time and then made the decision one day."[8]

Jolie says she, Pitt, and Maddox were in a hotel room, playing with cars on the floor when Maddox called him Dad. "We both heard it and didn't say anything and just looked at each other. So that was probably the most defining moment, when he decided that we would all be a family."[9]

Jolie and Pitt navigated through their budding relationship in closely-held privacy. Because they refused to even acknowledge there *was* a relationship for so long, entertainment and tabloid media attempted to fill in the blanks—with a little help from Aniston's friends. The picture that was painted was one of bad timing—while Jennifer wanted to start a family with Brad, "she was not willing to bring a baby into an unhappy marriage," said one friend. "She comes from a broken home herself and she knows that having a child is not the answer."[10]

Some movie-industry analysts wondered if the white hot media glare focused on Pitt and Jolie would hurt *Mr. and Mrs. Smith*, a dark comedy about a married couple who are, unbeknownst to each other, both professional assassins hired to kill each other. "Brad and I had a lot of fight scenes," Jolie says. "But that was good because we're very competitive in real life, so that made things very interesting."[11]

The studio need not have worried. *Mr. and Mrs. Smith* opened on June 7 and was a box office hit—the biggest of Jolie's career. Their on-screen chemistry was practically combustible.

Reviewer Constance Gorfinkle enthused, "Brad Pitt as John Smith and Angelina Jolie as Jane Smith are absolutely perfect. In fact, they may be the new Cary Grant and Katharine Hepburn, so wonderfully do they mesh, so ironic and confident are their attitudes. Just looking at them is a treat. Actually, Pitt hasn't been so well-cast since his stunning, brief encounter in *Thelma & Louise*."[12]

In July, 2005, Pitt and Jolie expanded their new family when she adopted a five-month-old AIDS orphan from Ethiopia. She and Pitt named their daughter Zahara Marley Jolie—Zahara is a Swahili name meaning flower. Just as with Maddox, Jolie initially adopted as a single parent since she and Pitt weren't married. Later Pitt legally adopted Zahara and Maddox and their last names changed to Jolie-Pitt.

While in Ethiopia preparing to bring Zahara home, Jolie explained, "My son is in love with Africa, so he has been asking for an African brother or sister . . . I want to create a rainbow family," she added, "that's children of different religions and cultures, from different countries."[13]

However vague Jolie may have been about when exactly her friendship with Pitt turned romantic, one thing is now sure: sometime around September 2005, she became pregnant—Maddox and Zahara were going to get a sibling. On January 11, 2006, Jolie and Pitt finally acknowledged they were a couple when they announced her pregnancy through Pitt's publicist (Jolie does not employ a personal publicist). They also confirmed reports that Brad was in the process of legally adopting Maddox and Zahara.

Jolie acknowledged the pregnancy was planned, meaning the woman who always said she wasn't that interested in giving birth clearly had a change of heart. "Before I met Brad, I always said I was happy never to have a child biologically. He told me he hadn't given up that thought. Then, a few months after Z came home, I saw Brad with her and Mad, and I realized how much he loved them; that a biological child would not in any way be a threat. So I said, *I want to try*."[14]

The announcement came while Jolie was filming *The Good Shepherd* opposite Matt Damon. The film, directed by Robert De Niro, tells the story of the CIA's beginning through Damon's character. Jolie plays his troubled wife, Clover, who deals with the stress of her husband's covert life by becoming an alcoholic. The character was a departure for Jolie, who is not known for playing weak women. Jolie admits she has little in common with Clover except that they are both mothers. Jolie characterizes her acting in *The Good Shepherd* as a study in restraint. Her character lived in a time where it was expected that she maintain a certain kind of decency and composure, regardless of whether she was unhappy or wanted out of the marriage. Jolie couldn't identify with that type of restraint, so she tried to stay grounded to her through their common bond of motherhood.[15]

Jolie also had a hard time envisioning herself with someone so secretive. "I've never had that in my life 'cause I've always married artists, and they're always talkative and an expressive bunch. So that was bizarre. But I think that was part of the character that was interesting, because she did feel lost and trapped and confused. I do see her in the end as being as strong as a woman could be in that time, but I did like that there were many things about her that were broken. I don't often get to play that part."[16]

And now that she was a mother of two with another on the way, the number of roles she would take had diminished. "The thing now that makes the big choice is, how long is it shooting?" she said in 2006, "Because I don't think I've shot more than seven weeks on a movie in two years. I need to make sure I have time with my kids."[17]

As Jolie's pregnancy progressed, the media interest in the couple raged on. In order to get away from the British and American paparazzi, Jolie and Pitt decided to sequester themselves in the remote, African nation of Namibia, an impoverished country of 1.8 million. They traveled to the country in mid-April to await the birth of their child, staying at the Burning Shore Beach Lodge resort. British tabloids reported that the star couple had demanded Namibia ban journalists from entering the country but tourism minister Leon Jooste said the decision to restrict visas was made by government officials.

"Things were getting really out of hand because of paparazzi," Jooste says. "But they never asked for anything; they simply said to me: *Listen, things are getting a bit out of hand.* So I spoke to a bunch of people within the government. For a small country like ours, with a small economy and a growing tourism industry, this is of major marketing value for us."[18]

When several photographers were expelled from Namibia in early May, some human rights groups accused Namibia of breaking the law. Prime Minister Nahas Angula shrugged off the criticism. "This lady is expecting," he said. You guys are harassing her . . . Harassment is not allowed in Namibia."[19]

Shiloh Nouvel Jolie-Pitt was born via C-section at the Cottage Hospital in Swakopmund on May 27, 2006, weighing in at 7 pounds. Jolie describes the hospital as a cottage. "I don't think there was anybody else in the hospital . . . it ended up being the greatest thing. We had wonderful doctors and nurses. It was lovely, very personal."[20] She had an American doctor attending her who worked with the Namibian physicians.

Jolie says they picked the name Shiloh because that was the name her parents would have called their first child if her mother had not miscarried. "My father had been shooting in Georgia and that was the most southern name [my parents] could come up with," she revealed. "It's a name I always liked. I used to go under it in hotels: Shiloh Baptist. I'd gone under it when [Brad] called hotel rooms where I was staying."[21]

Jolie admitted she had a few moments of terror during the birth. "You know, because you're there for the birth, which I wasn't for my first two kids, you're just suddenly terrified that they're not gonna take a first breath. That was my whole focus; I just wanted to hear her cry."[22]

People magazine snagged the first published pictures of Shiloh for a reported $4 million, the proceeds of which were donated by Pitt and Jolie to children's charities in Africa. Prior to Shiloh's birth, Jolie did an interview with the *Today* show while in Namibia to promote the need for better education in the world's poorest areas.

"I just think, especially my daughter, there's no possible way she would have gone to school. She is so smart and so strong. And her potential as a woman one day is great," she says. "Hopefully, she will be active in her country and in her continent when she's older. And because she'll have a good education, she'll be able to do that much more."[23]

Jolie was not just an advocate, but a benefactor. She revealed she gave a third of her income to charity, joking, "Yeah, well, I had a stupid income for what I do."[24]

In July 2006, Jolie signed on to her first post-Shiloh film, *A Mighty Heart*, about the real-life kidnapping and beheading of *Wall Street Journal* reporter Daniel Pearl. Jolie plays Pearl's pregnant wife, Mariane. Brad Pitt was executive producer. Ironically, Mariane Pearl started talking to Pitt about making the movie before he and Jolie began dating.

Pearl had contacted Jolie and suggested they get together for a play-date after reading an interview Jolie gave about being a single mom. "Her instincts were right," Angelina says, "we did have so much in common. And all the kids are great friends now. Zahara is madly in love with Adam," she adds, referring to Mariane's son.[25]

Jolie says their friendship, and Pitt's involvement, was a bit nerve-wracking. "Having your partner producing can sound like a good idea but can also make the pressure much harder; to do right by him and by Mariane became a pressure that I lost sleep over," she said.[26]

In November 2006, Jolie and Pitt quietly visited Vietnam where they visited the Tam Binh orphanage near Ho Chi Minh City and started the paperwork to adopt a three-year-old boy. The following March, Jolie went back to take custody of her newest son, named Pax Thien.

"Pax is a great kid," she says. "When we first met him, we thought he was really shy and quiet but after two days at home we've discovered that he is one of the loudest members of the family."[27] Like Maddox, Pax has a language tutor to keep him fluent in his native languages.

Jolie acknowledges that adopting a toddler is more challenging than adopting an infant, and that she wouldn't have been ready to take on that challenge earlier. "But I felt now our home was stable, and I could balance that," She said. Pax cried a lot the first couple days, but then he settled down and Jolie suspected that "I think he got used to the reality that somebody loves you and that's what a mommy is."[28]

The decision to adopt an Asian child was made with their other adopted children in mind. "Something changed for me with Shiloh," Jolie says. "We had Mad and Z, and neither looked like Mommy or Daddy. Then suddenly somebody in the house looked like Mommy and Daddy. It became clear to us that it might be important to have somebody around who is similar to the other children so they have a connection. Mad's been very excited that his brother is from Asia."[29]

Tragically for Jolie, her mom never got to meet Pax. Marceline Bertrand died January 27, 2007 after a seven-year battle with ovarian and breast cancer. She was only 56 years old. Her death hit Angelina and her brother James hard. Jolie lost weight and suffered from impromptu crying jags. Despite her grief, Angelina was grateful that her mom lived long enough to see both her children happy. "You almost get the feeling she held on until it was okay," Jolie commented.[30]

Bertrand died at Cedar Sinai in Los Angeles. "I had to be responsible for getting the morgue to pick her body up," said Jolie. "All I have to do is remind myself that she's my best girlfriend and she's not in any more pain. I'm so happy for her. As much as I miss her, I'm a good enough friend not to have wanted her to stay in pain any longer."[31]

In January 2008, rumors began swirling that Jolie was pregnant again. While at the Cannes film festival in May, she confirmed she was expecting twins. Instead of returning to Africa, for this pregnancy the Jolie-Pitt clan awaited the birth at a rented house in the south of France. Typically, her every move is reported in minute detail, prompting Jolie to look forward to the day their celebrity fades. "By the time the kids are old enough to really understand all this, hopefully we will be less in the public eye. We will do fewer films, we will not be that couple."[32] Two weeks prior to her scheduled C-section, Jolie was admitted to Lenval Hospital to rest and for observation. Late in the evening on July 12, she gave birth to twins—Knox Leon and Vivienne Marcheline—born one minute apart. Her obstetrician, Dr. Michel Sussmann, delivered the babies.

In August 2008, Pitt and Jolie sold the first pictures of their twins for $14 million to *People* and the British tabloid *Hello!* The money was funneled to the Jolie-Pitt Foundation, which provides humanitarian aid around the world, such as its $1 million donation in June 2008 to help children in Iraq.

So far, though, Jolie's work load remains steady, with *Kung Fu Panda*, *Wanted*, and *Changeling* released in 2008. "I take films very seriously," she says. "I love being able to tell a good story or just to entertain. It's just that at the end of the day, when I die, I feel that the more significant contribution to have made would be to save a life or change a law that's going to affect people and their children and their country and their rights in the future." Also, for as much as she loves acting, being a mother comes first. "I want to raise children who will be good people and be a positive influence in this world. Everything else I have been able to do in my life through entertainment has certainly helped facilitate the other."[33]

One thing that's not a priority for Jolie, or Pitt, is marriage. Pitt has said he won't get married again until all people, including same-sex couples, can legally marry. "We both have been married before, so it's not marriage that's necessarily kept some people together," Jolie says. "We are legally bound to our children, not to each other, and I think that's the most important thing."[34]

NOTES

1. Michelle Lopez, "I Just Naturally Don't Rely on Men," *Mail on Sunday*, January 2, 2005, http://www.highbeam.com/doc/1P2-2497274.html.

2. Ibid.

3. Ibid.

4. BBCNews.com, "Pitt and Aniston Announce Split," January 8, 2005, http://news.bbc.co.uk/2/low/entertainment/4156907.stm.

5. Jonathan Van Meter, "The Bold and the Beautiful," *Vogue*, January 2007, http://www.style.com/vogue/feature/121206/page2.html.

6. Ibid.

7. Ibid.

8. Ibid.

9. Stephen M. Silverman, "Angelina Jolie: How Brad Pitt & I Fell in Love," December 12, 2006, http://www.people.com/people/article/0,,20004139,00.html.

10. Nicole Lampert, "End of the Fairy Tale," *Daily Mail*, January 10, 2005, http://www.highbeam.com/doc/1P2-2497701.html.

11. "Good Golly, Ms. Jolie," *The Birmingham Post*, June 8, 2005, http://www.highbeam.com/doc/1G1-133070926.html.

12. Constance Gorfinkle, "*Mr. and Mrs. Smith* Movie Review," *The Patriot Ledger*, June 10, 2005, http://www.highbeam.com/doc/1P2-9431408.html.

13. Nicole Lampert, "Angelina Jolie Adopts an AIDS Orphan Girl from Ethiopia," *Daily Mail*, July 7, 2005, http://www.highbeam.com/doc/1P2-2564869.html.

14. Readers' Digest http://www.laineygossip.com/Angelina_Jolie_Brad_Pitt_I_Buy_What_She_Sells.aspx. See also Sara Davidson, "Mama," *Readers' Digest*, July 2007, http://www.women24.com/Readers_Digest/Display/ReadersDigest_Article/0,,938-983_14647,00.html.

15. Liz Braun, "The Incandescent Miss Jolie," *Toronto Sun*, December 17, 2006, http://jam.canoe.ca/Movies/Artists/J/Jolie_Angelina/2006/12/17/2841436.html.

16. Ibid.

17. Ibid.

18. Robin Stummer, "To Brad and Angelina: A C-section," *The Independent on Sunday*, May 28, 2006, http://www.highbeam.com/doc/1P2-2017363.html.

19. Ibid.

20. Ibid.

21. Rich Cohen, "A Woman in Full," *Vanity Fair*, July 2008, http://www.vanityfair.com/culture/features/2008/07/jolie200807.

22. Angelina Jolie, interviewed by Anderson Cooper, *Anderson Cooper's 360*, CNN, June 16, 2006.

23. Angelina Jolie, *Today*, NBC, April 27, 2006.

24. Ibid.

25. Emily Fromm, "Angelina Jolie: 'I Was Nervous' About Playing Mariane Pearl,'" *People*, April 30, 2007, http://www.people.com/people/article/0,,20037287,00.html.

26. "Mother Angelina," *Evening Standard*, June 14, 2007, http://www.highbeam.com/doc/1P2-7469981.html.

27. "Angelina Jolie," *Marie Claire*, July 2007, http://justjared.buzznet.com/2007/06/05/angelina-jolie-marie-claire-july-2007/.

28. Ibid.

29. Ibid.

30. Readers' Digest http://www.laineygossip.com/Angelina_Jolie_Brad_Pitt_I_Buy_What_She_Sells.aspx

31. Cohen, "A Woman in Full."

32. "Mother Angelina," *Evening Standard*.

33. Ibid.

34. Van Meter, "The Bold and the Beautiful."

SELECTED BIBLIOGRAPHY

"50 Most Beautiful People," *People*, March 31, 1998.

Access Hollywood. Broadcast August 1, 2002.

Anderson Cooper's 360. CNN Broadcast June 16, 2006.

"Angelina in Love." *Talk* (June/July 2000). Available at: http://fansites.holly
wood.com/~ajolie/int6.html.

Angelina Jolie Biography. People.com. Available at: http://www.people.com/peo
ple/angelina_jolie/biography.

"Angelina Jolie—Gone in 60 Seconds." beatboxbetty.com. Available at: http://
www.beatboxbetty.com/celebetty/angelinajolie/angelinajolie2/angelina
jolie2.htm.

"Angelina Jolie." *Marie Claire* (July 2007). Available at: http://justjared.buzznet.
com/2007/06/05/angelina-jolie-marie-claire-july-2007/.

Anderson, Diane. "'Tis the Season to Be Jolie." *Girlfriends* (December 1997).
Available at: http://members.fortunecity.com/foxdm/id88.htm.

Angeli, Michael. "Tres Jolie." *Movieline* (February 1999). Available at: http://
members.fortunecity.com/jamralla/angel/MovielineFeb99.htm.

Archerd, Army. "*Wallace* Exiled from Alabama." *Variety* (January 17,
1997). Available at: http://www.variety.com/article/VR1117863009.
html?categoryid=2&cs=1.

Archerd, Army. "Just for Variety." *Variety* (February 25, 1997).

Arnold, Chuck. "Chatter." *People* (May 3, 1999). Available at: http://www.peo
ple.com/people/archive/article/0,,20128100,00.html

Ascher-Walsh, Rebecca, et al. "Fall Movie Preview: October." *Entertainment
Weekly* (August 22, 1997).

Avins, Mimi. "A Sleeping Beauty: Gia Carangi Had It All, Or So It Seemed in the *Cosmo* Cover Photos of Her." *Los Angeles Times* (January 29, 1998).

Barnes, Harper. "Tripping on the Net: Sophomoric Is the Sum of It." *St. Louis Post-Dispatch* (September 15, 1995).

BBC News.com. "Pitt and Aniston announce split" (January 8, 2005). Available at: http://news.bbc.co.uk/2/low/entertainment/4156907.stm.

Bergman, Anne. "A Proverbial Adventurer." *Los Angeles Times* (November 17, 1999).

Blanchet, Cate. "Pushing Tin." *Evening Standard* (October 26, 1999). Available at: http://www.geocities.com/hollywood/Land/9730/tinarticle1.html.

Boleyn, Alison. "Celebrity Profile: Angelina Jolie." *Marie Claire* (February 2000).

Braun, Liz. "Billy Bob Thornton Gets His Jolies." *Ottawa Sun* (June 26, 2000).

Braun, Liz. "The Incandescent Miss Jolie." *Toronto Sun* (December 17, 2006). Available at: http://jam.canoe.ca/Movies/Artists/J/Jolie_Angelina/2006/12/17/2841436.html.

Cohen, Rich. "A Woman in Full." *Rolling Stone* (July 2008).

Czyzselska, Jane. "Jenny Shimizu & Rebecca Loos: What's The Story?" *Diva* (November 2005). Available at: http://Www.Divamag.Co.Uk/Diva/Features.Asp?Aid=287&S=1.

Davidson, Sara. "Mama." *Readers' Digest* (July 2007). Available at: http://www.women24.com/Readers_Digest/Display/ReadersDigest_Article/0,,938-983_14647,00.html.

Dawson, Angela. "Angelina Jolie: Rewing Her Engines." *Newsday* (June 13, 2000).

Deitch Rohrer, Trish. "Dangerous Beauties: Winona Ryder and .Angelina Jolie Walk on the Wild Side." *Premiere* (October 1999). Available at: http://www.hollywood.com/news/Winona_Interrupted/311849.

Dretzka, Gary. "Angelina Jolie Warily Regards Rising Fame." *Chicago Tribune* (September 4, 1996), p. 5.

D'Souza, Christa. "Do You Wanna Be in My Gang? Actor Jonny Lee Miller is Mr. Cool." *Daily Telegraph* (March 17, 2000).

Edel, Raymond A. "People." *Record* (April 15, 1999).

Essex, Andrew. "Girl Uncorrupted: Razor-Sharp Turns in *Gia* and *Wallace* Got Her Noticed." *Entertainment Weekly* (November 5, 1999).

Feinstein, Sharon. "My sister Angelina's secret sadness." *Mail on Sunday* (March 25, 2007). Available at: http://www.highbeam.com/doc/1P2–13554319.html.

Fromm, Emily. "Angelina Jolie: 'I Was Nervous About Playing Mariane Pearl.'" *People* (April 30, 2007). Available at: http://www.people.com/people/article/0,,20037287,00.html.

Garner, Jack. "Jolie's Performance in *Playing by Heart* Is Drawing Attention." Gannett News Service (January 21, 1999).

George Wallace production notes. Available at: http://alt.tnt.tv/movies/tntorigi
    nals/wallace/prod.credits.notes.html.

Germain, David. "Angelina Jolie Brushes Off Bad Press." *Dallas MorningNews*
    (June 11, 2000).

Gilbey, Ryan. "A Cat with Nine Former Lives." *Independent* (May 2, 1996). Avail-
    able at: http://www.highbeam.com/doc/1P2–4786214.html.

"Girl Uncorrupted." EntertainmentWeekly.com. Available at: http://members.
    fortunecity.com/foxdm/id68.htm.

"Girl, Uninhibited." *Maxim* (June 2000). Available at: http://team-jolie.com/
    press_magazines2000.php?subaction=showfull&id=1196285322&archive
    =&start_from=&ucat=32&.

Gleiberman, Owen. "Pushing Tin." *Entertainment Weekly* (April 23, 1999). Avail-
    able at: http://www.ew.com/ew/article/0,,64000,00.html.

Gleiberman, Owen. Review of *Girl, Interrupted. Entertainment Weekly* (January 7,
    2000).

Golden Globe Awards. Broadcast January 18, 1998, on NBC.

Goldman, Steve. "Angelina Jolie." *Total Film* (March 2000).

"Good Golly, Ms. Jolie." *The Birmingham Post* (June 8, 2005). Available at: http://
    www.highbeam.com/doc/1G1–133070926.html.

Gorfinkle, Constance. "Mr and Mrs Smith movie review." *The Patriot Ledger*
    (June 10, 2005). Available at: http://www.highbeam.com/doc/1P2–9431408.
    html.

Graham, Caroline. "Shooting from the Lips." *Mail on Sunday* (August 3, 2003).
    Available at: http://www.highbeam.com/doc/1P2–2339208.html.

Greppi, Michele. "Gia: Supermodel in the Raw." *New York Post* (January 31,
    1998).

Hardy, Ernest. "*Hell's Kitchen:* No Escape from the Past, Especially a Criminal
    One." *New York Times* (December 3, 1999).

Harrison, Eric. "The Many Faces of Voight . . ." *Los Angeles Times* (January 22,
    1999), p. 2.

Heckman, Don. "Jolie Breathes Life into Gia's Tragic Tale." *Los Angeles Times*
    (January 31, 1998).

Heisler, Bob. "Talk It Up." *Newsday* (January 31, 1999).

Heyman, J. D. "Angelina Jolie Marries Billy Bob Thornton." *Us* (April 22, 2000).

Hobson, Louis B. "Pushing Her Luck: Angelina Jolie's Full-Tilt Existence." *Cal-
    gary Sun* (April 18, 1999). Available at: http://jam.canoe.ca/Movies/Art
    ists/J/Jolie_Angelina/1999/04/18/759417.html.

Hobson, Louis B. "An Old Soul." *London Free Press* (April 20, 1999).

Hobson, Louis B. "Angelina Jolie is no Angel." *Ottawa Sun* (August 30, 1999).
    Available at: http://jam.canoe.ca/Movies/Artists/J/Jolie_Angelina/1999/
    08/30/759416.html.

Hobson, Louis B. "Jolie Intense to the Bone." *Calgary Sun* (October 31, 1999).

Hobson, Louis B. "Dark Angel: Angelina Jolie has a decidedly sinister side." *Calgary Sun* (November 4, 1999). Available at: http://members.fortunecity.com/ajonline/information/articles/022.htm.

Hobson, Louis B. "You go, girls." Available at: http://jam.canoe.ca/Movies/Artists/R/Ryder_Winona/2000/01/09/761355.html.

Hobson, Louis B. "Going by Murphy's law." Jam.com. Available at: http://jam.canoe.ca/Movies/Artists/M/Murphy_Brittany/2000/01/09/760428.html.

Hobson, Louis B. "Angie, Committed." *Edmonton Sun* (January 9, 2000).

Hobson, Louis B. "Jolie's Rocky Relationships." *Calgary Sun* (January 9, 2000). Available at: http://www.jonnyleemiller.co.uk/angelinajolie.html.

Hobson, Louis B. "The Jolly Life of Angelina." Available at: http://jam.canoe.ca/Movies/Artists/J/Jolie_Angelina/2003/07/20/759421.html.

Holt, Jessica. "'Girl' Offers Comfort for Misunderstood." *Daily Bruin* (January 10, 2000). 'http://ryder.fan-sites.org/2000january10_dailybruinonline.htm.

Inside Edition interview. Broadcast July 21, 2003.

Interview with Angelina Jolie. www.beatboxbetty.com (May 23, 2000). Available at: http://www.beatboxbetty.com/celebetty/angelinajolie/angelinajolie/angelinajolie.htm.

Interview with Jonny Lee Miller. *Just 17*. Available at: http://members.tripod.com/~Odessa-X/just17.html.

"Is Angelina Jolie The It Girl For The 21st Century?" *Jezebel* (February 2000). Available at: http://angelanna3.tripod.com/interviews2000/id9.html.

Ivry, Bob. "A Man and His Times." *Record* (August 24, 1997).

Ivry, Bob. "Relatively Secret." *Record* (April 25, 1999). ' http://www.highbeam.com/doc/1P1–24208016.html.

James, Christine. "'Dancing' Queen Angelina Jolie Gets Constructive in *Dancing About Architecture*." Available at: www.boxoffice.com.

"Jenny Shimizu: From Grease Monkey to Supermodel." *Curve* (September 1996).

"Jonny Lee Miller and Angelina Jolie: The Happy Couple." *Empire* (June 1996). Available at: http://www.jonnyleemiller.co.uk/angelinajolie.html.

Jucaud, Dany. "And the Devil Created Angelina Jolie." Paris Match (February 17, 2000). Available at: http://angelanna3.tripod.com/interviews2000/id11.html.

Kaplan, James. "Holy Moly. It's Angelina Jolie." *Allure* (March 1999). Available at: http://www.wutheringjolie.com/nuke/modules.php?name=Content&pa=showpage&pid=360.

Kelleher, Terry. "Picks and Pans: Tube." *People* (August 25, 1997).

Kilian, Michael. "HBO Presents Wild, Sad Story Of Supermodel Gia Carangi." *Chicago Tribune* (January 26, 1998).

King, Susan. "Don't Hate Her Because She's Lucky." *Los Angeles Times* (August 24, 1996).

Kirkland, Bruce. "Winona Ryder's Talking Crazy." Available at: http://jam.canoe. ca/Movies/Artists/R/Ryder_Winona/1999/12/20/761356.html.

Kirkland, Bruce. "She's Got Game." Available at: http://jam.canoe.ca/Movies/ Artists/J/Jolie_Angelina/2001/06/10/759412.html.

Kirkland, Bruce. "In Praise of Angelina Jolie." Available at: http://jam.canoe. ca/Movies/Artists/J/Jolie_Angelina/2001/06/15/759410.html.

Kirkland, Bruce. "The New Angelina Jolie." Available at: http://jam.canoe.ca/ Movies/Artists/J/Jolie_Angelina/2003/10/19/759420.html.

Kizis, Deanna. "Truth and Consequences." *Harper's Bazaar* (November 1999). Available at: http://fansites.hollywood.com/~ajolie/int15.html.

Lampert, Nicole. "End of the Fairy Tale." *Daily Mail* (January 10, 2005). Available at: http://www.highbeam.com/doc/1P2–2497701.html

Lampert, Nicole. "Angelina Jolie adopts an Aids orphan girl from Ethiopia." *Daily Mail* (July 7, 2005). Available at: http://www.highbeam.com/doc/1P2–2564869.html.

Lanie, Tricia. "Girl Talk: Hollywood's Actresses Are Abuzz About the Film Version of *Girl, Interrupted.*" *Entertainment Weekly* (October 23, 1998).

Late Night with Conan O'Brien. NBC. Broadcast January 29, 1998.

Late Night with Conan O'Brien. NBC. Broadcast January 13, 2000.

Lee, Luaine. "Angelina Jolie is a mother in *Alexander* and in real life." Knight-Ridder (November 5, 2004). Available at: http://www.highbeam.com/doc/ 1G1–124647029.html.

Levy, Maury Z. "Cover Girl." *Philadelphia* (January1980).

Longsdorf, Amy. "Angelina Jolie as the Ill-Fated Supermodel in the Biopic *Gia.*" *Playboy* (May 2000).

Longsdorf, Amy. "Woman on the Verge." *Playboy.* Available at: http://www.play boy.co.uk/page/WomenOnTheVerge/0,,11569~766428,00.html.

Lopez, Michelle. "I Justt Naturally Don't Rely on Men." Mail on Sunday (January 2, 2005). Available at: http://www.highbeam.com/doc/1P2-2497274. html.

Mackenzie, Drew, and Ivor Davis. "I'm Both Sinister and Soft." *Woman's Day* (Australia) (April 17, 2000). Available at: http://zone.ee/daart/ar42.html.

Mann, Barry. "I Have No One to Have Sex With." NW (January 24, 2000).

Mansfield, Stephanie. "Oscar-Winning Actress Angelina Jolie Says She's Putting Her Wild Past Behind Her." *USA Weekend* (June 11, 2000). Available at: http://www.usaweekend.com/00_issues/000611/000611jolie.html.

Martin, Ed. "Gutsy Gia Goes Beyond Skin Deep." *USA Today* (January 30, 1998).

Mathews, Jack. "Don't Quit Your Day Job, David." *Newsday* (October 17, 1997).

Medved, Michael. "Playing God." *New York Post*. Available at: http://members. tripod.com/~GiaLegs/articles-pgod.html.

Millar, John. "It felt so sexy to be Colin"s mum." *Sunday Mail* (December 5, 2004). Available at: http://www.highbeam.com/doc/1G1–125808161.html.

Miller, Prairie. "Interview with Jon Voight." *Star Interviews* (January 1, 1998). Available at: http://www.highbeam.com/doc/1P1–20559900.html.

Miller, Prairie. "A Simple Plan: Interview with Billy Bob Thornton." *Star Interviews* (January 1, 1998).

"Mother Angelina." *Evening Standard* (June 14, 2007). Available at: http://www. highbeam.com/doc/1P2–7469981.html.

Nash, Alanna. "Gia: Fashion Victim." *Entertainment Weekly* (January 16, 1998). Available at: http://www.ew.com/ew/article/0,,281498,00.html.

Nicholson, William F. "'Terrible Lawyer' Keeps Wheels of Justice Turning." *USA Today* (August 13, 1998), p. 4D.

Norris, Chris. "Say Goodbye to the Brooding Gen-Xer: Winona Ryder Has Grown into a Woman of Impeccable Taste." *In Style* (January 2, 2000).

"Now Our Mel's Starring in the Crying Game." *Sunday Mail* (February 27, 2000).

O'Neil, Oliver. "The wild and wacky world of Angelina Jolie, Tomb Raider." Planet Syndication. Available at: http://www.unreel.co.uk/features/feature angelinajoliepage3.cfm.

"On the Move: Name Dropper Not Billing Herself as a Voight." *People* (July 8, 1996). Available at: http://www.people.com/people/archive/article/0,,20 141730,00.html.

Osborne, Bert. "Interview with Angelina Jolie." *Jezebel* (February 2000).

Parnes, Francine. "The Sweet Face of the Future." *Daily Telegraph* (May 26, 1999).

Pearlman, Cindy. "Angelina Jolie far from angelic." *Chicago Sun-Times* (April 18, 1999). Available at: http://www.highbeam.com/doc/1P2–4489196.html.

Pearlman, Cindy. "A Jolie Good Time." *Daily Telegraph* (June 10, 2000).

Pearlman, Cindy. "Counting Blessings." *Chicago Sun-Times* (November 25, 2003). Available at: http://www.highbeam.com/doc/1P2–1513012.html.

Penguin Press Release (1994). Available at: http://www.robtee.com/books/Fox fire_Confessions-of-a-Girl-Gang.htm.

Peveref, Geoff. "*Girl* an Unsatisfying Minor Interruption." *Toronto Star* (December 21, 1999).

Pinsker, Beth. "Foxfire Extinguishes Oates Novel's Spark." *Dallas Morning News* (August 26, 1996).

Press Release from MGM. Available at: http://209.85.141.104/search?q=cache: UNyBClUkShAJ:www.uncle.com/shake.html+We+don%E2%80%99t+a pprove+of+their+trashing+our+Web+site,+but+we+are+thoroughly+im pressed+by+their+creativity+and+ingenuity&hl=en&ct=clnk&cd=2& gl=us.

Production Notes, Universal Studios (November 1999). Available at: http:// www.thebonecollector.com/crimelab.html.

Pushing Tin production notes (April 1999). Available at: http://www.cinemare view.com/production.asp?prodid=556.

Readers' Digest. Available at: http://www.laineygossip.com/Angelina_Jolie_ Brad_Pitt_I_Buy_What_She_Sells.aspx

Ressner, Jeffery. "Rebel Without a Pause." *Time* (January 24, 2000). Available at: http://www.time.com/time/magazine/article/0,9171,37644,00.html.

Reynolds, Mark. "Angelina's troubles are all my fault sobs Voight." *Daily Mail* (August 3, 2002). Available at: http://www.highbeam.com/doc/1P2–22 47922.html.

Richardson, John H. "Angelina Jolie and the Torture of Fame." *Esquire* (February 2000).

Sager, Mike. "Women We Love: Angelina Jolie." *Esquire* (November 1, 2004). Available at: http://www.highbeam.com/doc/1G1–123637183.html.

Sandell, Laurie. "Reckless Angel." *Biography* (October 1999).

Scaduto, Anthony. "Flash! The Latest Entertainment News and More." *Newsday* (September 4, 1996).

Scavullo, Francesco. *Scavullo Women.* New York: Harper and Row, 1982.

Schneider, Karen S. "Girl, Undaunted." *People* (June 25, 2001). Available at: http://www.people.com/people/archive/article/0,,20134761,00.html.

Seymour, Gene. "Disorder in the Ward: A Memoir of a Teen Mental Institution." *Newsday* (December 21, 1999).

Shapiro, Erik. Letter to the Editor. *Entertainment Weekly* (November 26, 1999).

Silverman, Stephen M. "U.N. Honoring Goodwill Angelina Jolie." *People* (August 22, 2001).

Silverman, Stephen M. "Jolie Accepts U.N. Ambassador Post. *People* (August 28, 2001). Available at: http://www.people.com/people/article/0,,622486,00. html.

Silverman, Stephen M. "Angelina Jolie: $1 Mil to Refugees." *People* (September 28, 2001).

Silverman, Stephen M. "Angelina Jolie Airs Colorful Past on TV." *People* (July 9, 2003). Available at: http://www.people.com/people/article/0,,626414,00. html.

Silverman, Stephen M. "Jolie Talks About 'Borders' and Babies." *People* (October 23, 2003).

Silverman, Stephen M. "Angelina Jolie: How Brad Pitt & I Fell in Love." (December 12, 2006). Available at: http://www.people.com/people/article/ 0,,20004139,00.html.

Simon, Brent. "Girl, Conflicted." *Entertainment Today* (January 2000).

Smith, Liz. "The New Courtney." *Newsday* (August 24, 1997).

Snead, Elizabeth. "Gia Taps Angelina Jolie's Wild Side." *USA Today* (January 29, 1998). Available at: http://members.tripod.com/~GiaLegs/interviews.html.

Snead, Elizabeth. "These Sibs Are Close, But Not That Close!" *USA Today* (April 7, 2000).

Snead, Elizabeth. "Jolie Embraces Love, Fame for More than 60 Seconds." *USA Today* (June 8, 2000).

Spice, Kate. "Stand and Deliver, It's Jonny Lee Miller." *Minx* (April 1998).

Stenze, Jack. "Get Reel: Can Angelina Jolie Make Lara Croft Soar on Screen?" *Entertainment Weekly* (April 14, 2000).

Strickler, Jeff. "Actors Hope They Can Hack It: Cyber-Film Stars Faked Computer Skills." *Minneapolis Star Tribune* (September 10, 1995).

Stoynoff, Natasha. "She's Having a Jolie Time Kissing." *Toronto Sun* (June 18, 2000).

Stummer, Robin. "To Brad and Angelina: a C-section." *The Independent on Sunday* (May 28, 2006). Available at: http://www.highbeam.com/doc/1P2-2017363.html.

Sutton, Larry, Ken Baker, and Champ Clark. "Ark de Triumph: Jon Voight Sets Sail on T.V. as Noah." *People* (May 3, 1999). Available at: http://members.tripod.com/~Monkees23/jvoight/jvpeopl.html.

Tauber, Michelle. "And Baby Makes Two." *People* (August 4, 2003). Available at: http://www.people.com/people/archive/article/0,,20140693,00.html.

Te Koha, Nui. "Psychiatric Ward Stay No 'Jolie' Matter." *Sunday Mail* (May 21, 2000).

"That Girl: An Interview with Actress Angelina Jolie." Drdrew.com. Ray Pride (2000). Available at: http://www.drdrew.com/DrewLive/article.asp?id=406.

Thomas, Kevin. "Love Is All There Is: Tale of Young Love Takes Aim at an Older Audience." *Los Angeles Times* (March 28, 1997). Available at: http://www.chicagotribune.com/topic/cl-movie970328-5,1,692960.story.

Thompson, Bob. "The Many Faces of Angelina." *Toronto Sun* (April 11, 1999).

Thompson, Bob. "Johnny Be Good: Actor, Writer and Producer Cusack Is Still Learning." *Edmonton Sun* (April 20, 1999).

Thompson, David. "Drive Us Wild, Angelina." *Salon* (June 14, 2000).

Today. NBC. Broadcast October 23, 1997.

Today. NBC. Broadcast April 27, 2006.

The Tonight Show with Jay Leno. NBC. Broadcast January 29, 1998.

Udovitch, Mimi. "The Devil in Miss Jolie." *Rolling Stone* (August 19, 1999). Available at: http://www.rollingstone.com/news/story/5939518/the_devil_in_miss_jolie.

Van Meter, Jonathan. "The Bold and the Beautiful." *Vogue* (January 7, 2008). Available at: http://www.style.com/vogue/feature/121206/popup/slideshow7. html.

Vigoa, Arlene. "And the First Time Nominees Are . . ." *USA Today* (March 20, 2000). Available at: http://www.usatoday.com/life/special/oscar2000/osc 05.htm.

Vognar, Chris. "On the Edge: Story of a Young Woman's Breakdown Is Both Dark and Illuminating." *Dallas Morning News* (January 14, 2000).

Voight, Jon. "Angelina Jolie." *Interview* (June 1977). Available at: http://www. highbeam.com/doc/1G1–19661469.html.

Weiner, Sherry. Interview with Angelina Jolie (1999). Available at: http://mem bers.fortunecity.com/ajonline/information/articles/012.htm.

Williams, Jeannie. "Voight a Dad Close to His Own 'Babies.'" *USA Today* (March 12, 1999).

Williams, Jeannie. "'Fair' Game After Oscar Party." *USA Today* (March 28, 2000).

Wong, Martin. "Review of *Foxfire*." A. *Magazine* (September 30, 1996).

Wuntch, Philip. "PLAYING GOD: Director's omnipotence smothers this thriller." *The Dallas Morning News* (October 17, 1997), p. 1C.

Wuntch, Phillip. "*The Bone Collector*: Villain Doesn't Have a Spine." *Dallas Morning News* (May 11, 1999).

INDEX

About the Author

KATHLEEN TRACY is a Los Angeles-based journalist. She is the author of over 20 titles, including *Elvis Presley: A Biography* (2006) and *Jennifer Lopez: A Biography* (2008).